Let God be God!

Brian William Warburton

Published by Brian William Warburton, 2023.

Dedicated to all those people who even through their own trials, still care and help others in need. The volunteers.

Let God be God!

Introduction.

The title may strike you as unusual. How can anyone possibly stop God from being who He is? That's a fair question. It may sound odd, but people can prevent God from being God in their lives. You will see the reason for the title as you read the book. Perhaps you're already aware of the answer, or you may already get the point. I encourage you to continue reading, for alertness is essential in these dangerous times. This book explores the source of our problems. It considers Christian and non-Christian perspectives. Are global and personal troubles rooted in humanity's inability to achieve peace? Or could there be a more profound spiritual issue? I can think immediately of three separate conflict areas. One area we should consider is how worldly influences often distract us with unimportant things. Second, I want to discuss the clandestine activities of sinister groups operating through intermediaries. Third, I believe that the greatest challenge we all face, especially Christians, is the battle within our own minds. There is the battle ground, it lies between our ears. Millennia ago, someone planted a seed in the human psyche. What that seed is and how it got planted will be investigated in the book. That seed, if unchecked, will become an insurmountable barrier between us and God. The seed is at the root of everyone's problems. This book explores the nature of the seed and how identifying it leads to successful extraction. To be victorious, you must be familiar with your adversary. Sun Tzu, the renowned ancient Chinese strategist, posited a proverb that emphasizes the importance of self-knowledge and understanding one's adversary: "In a hundred battles, you will never be in peril if you know the enemy and know yourself." Scripture speaks of two seeds, each holding symbolic meaning. Like a weed, the first seed sprouts and spoils the beautiful garden of life. The second seed sprouts and blooms, creating beauty, joy, and everlasting life in God's Garden. It's important to ensure the good seed thrives, not the weeds. The process of weeding is a never-ending task. Gardeners will understand this perfectly. You barely get the weeds cleared before they spring up again, much like problems in life.

I have walked with Jesus Christ for over forty years. Our journey commences with faith. Understanding God's plan for our future brings both freedom and contentment. The divine purpose is not to diminish the joy we experience in life, but rather to amplify it beyond our capacity to imagine. In this book, we'll delve into the universal relationship God extends to all people. It's important to note that God shows no partiality, as stated in Acts 10:34. Divine justice dictates that all people are treated equally. All individuals are invited into God's family. noting we are invited not forced against our will. Consequently, it's paramount to discern God's specific expectations. What steps are necessary to cultivate a profound and loving relationship with God, our Father? The only path to salvation is through faith in Jesus Christ, our redeemer.

All scriptural citations are drawn from the English Standard Version (ESV), unless otherwise specified. The words in italics are my own.

Chapter one.

The King is dead. Long live the King!

Exodus 15:18 "The LORD will reign forever and ever."

Let these profound words from ancient times sink in; He will reign (forever and ever). From our earthly perspective of time, it's sometimes hard to fully appreciate forever and ever. These words are translated from the two Hebrew words Olam (forever) and 'Ad (ever). Olam means "a remote period in the past," "a remote period in the future" or "in perpetuity." Sometimes this word is incorrectly translated world in English Bibles, but that was never the meaning of the Hebrew word. 'Ad comes from the root word 'adah which means to advance, pass by or come. It means past time, present time, and future time. We get the picture that the Lord not only (will) reign, but does and always has reigned.

If God is all-powerful, why do so many people disbelieve in God's existence? Then again, how many people are unaware of God or His plan for us? Humanity once had a close, loving relationship with God. It is our own lack of righteousness that separates humanity and God. God does not reject anyone who will come to him. Jesus removed the barrier that separates us from our God. Through the sacrifice of his blood, Jesus satisfied the demands of atonement by bearing the punishment we deserved for our sins, which is eternal separation from God. Jesus gave his life as the ultimate sacrifice. He broke down the barrier, allowing us to reunite with God. God offers us a choice between two different paths. The decision is ours.

Deuteronomy 30:19 I call heaven and earth to witness against you today, that I have set before you life and death, blessing and curse. Therefore choose life, that you and your offspring may live.

Choosing life implies a rebirth, not as a finite human, but as a divine offspring. Choosing to be a child of God necessitates active participation. Our heavenly Father has grand designs for our future. I am confident that if individuals were aware of the divine blessings awaiting them, they would readily embrace the opportunity to experience it today. The diversity of Christian denominations, each with its own set of beliefs, can be a source of confusion, especially for newcomers. Persistent and intense disagreements among Christians obscure the fundamental message of the Gospel. Why do individuals engage in protracted disputes over debatable issues when the Gospel message, the teachings of Jesus, is explicit and clear? Through an examination of the Bible's teachings, this book aims to illuminate God's present-day intentions and His plan for humanity. Everything we do should bring glory to God. Some years ago, I recall a prominent commentator stating that he found it impossible to believe in a God who demands worship. That shows a complete lack of understanding of God's word. To begin, God does not demand our worship. It's our choice. He presents us with life and death, and the choice is up to us. My second problem with that journalist's comment is this: Why wouldn't anyone want to worship God, who created everything for us with the power of his word? Why would you refuse to worship the God whom the angels of heaven praise? Why wouldn't you want to worship God, who provided us with everything for life and the chance to live in an paradise forever?

Studying God's Word will help us better understand what it means to "let God be God." You are likely familiar with the biblical account of two disciples walking together on the road to Emmaus; this passage holds great significance for me. Jesus' death deeply saddened the disciples, and their profound disappointment was a major topic of discussion. They crucified him, the man they believed was the messiah prophesied in the Torah, whom they had followed expecting he would become king of Israel. He is dead now. The crushing of their dreams of freedom in the promised land devastated them. As they walked along, lamenting their misfortune, a stranger suddenly appeared and joined them. The stranger's identity is still a mystery to them.

> Luke 24:13-16 "That very day two of them were going to a village named Emmaus, about seven miles from Jerusalem, 14 and they were talking with each other about all these things that had happened. 15 While they were talking and discussing together, Jesus himself drew near and went with them. 16 But their eyes were kept from recognizing him."

Jesus asked them "why do you look so sad?" this is their answer -

> Luke 24:18-21 "Then one of them, named Cleopas, answered him, "Are you the only visitor to Jerusalem who does not know the things that have happened there in these days?" 19 And he said to them, "What things?" And they said to him, "Concerning Jesus of Nazareth, a man who was a prophet mighty in deed and word before God and all the people, 20 and how our chief priests and rulers delivered him up to be condemned to death, and crucified him. 21 But we had hoped that he was the one to redeem Israel. Yes, and besides all this, it is now the third day since these things happened.""

At this time the Jewish people were under the oppressive rule of the occupying Roman army. The Romans occupied Israel from c 68 BC. The teachings of the Torah, which were central to the education of first-century Jewish boys, included the promise of a redeemer who would free them from the dominion of the gentile population in their land.

> Isaiah 9:4-7 "For the yoke of his burden, and the staff for his shoulder, the rod of his oppressor, you have broken as on the day of Midian. 5 For every boot of the tramping warrior in battle tumult and every garment rolled in blood will be burned as fuel for the fire. 6 For to us a child is born, to us a son is given; and the government shall be upon his shoulder, and his name shall be called Wonderful Counselor, Mighty God, Everlasting Father, Prince of Peace. 7 Of the increase of his government and of peace there will be no end, on the throne of David and over his kingdom, to establish it and to uphold it with justice and with righteousness from this time forth and forevermore. The zeal of the LORD of hosts will do this."

It's widely acknowledged today that this passage constitutes a prophecy concerning Jesus. He will eventually establish his throne, fulfilling the prophecy of Isaiah, but that is yet future, and only after the arrival of the Kingdom of God on earth. The Jewish people would have been offering prayers and yearning for the soon arrival of the redeemer King. Jesus' ministry to the Jewish people centered on the proclamation that the Kingdom of God was at hand. A significant number of people believed Jesus was the prophesied Messiah. The topic of conversation centered on Judea. Despite being identified as the anticipated King and savior mentioned in the Torah, Jesus has met a tragic end, leading to a sense of hopelessness. The two disciples, along with their companions, are deeply distressed. Jesus is dead. The contemporary world, for the most part, has disregarded the teachings of Jesus. Many people don't believe in God. Friedrich Nietzsche, the German philosopher and atheist, famously wrote, "God is dead." Nietzsche did not believe in the death of a God, because he didn't think one ever existed. He claimed that the idea of God was dead. The notion of life spontaneously generating from non-living matter is no longer something I accept. The two disciples make their way out of Jerusalem following the death of Jesus. Striding forward, enveloped in a state of despondency, their eyes cast downward. At that time, they were unaware that the death of Jesus had been prophesied millennia earlier. The resurrected Jesus approached and walked alongside them. Jesus explained to the two disciples that the scriptures affirm it necessary for the Redeemer to come first as a sacrificial atonement for their sins.

> Luke 24:25-27 "And he said to them, "O foolish ones, and slow of heart to believe all that the prophets have spoken! 26 Was it not necessary that the Christ should suffer these things and enter into his glory?" 27 And beginning with Moses and all the Prophets, he interpreted to them in all the Scriptures the things concerning himself."

The Bible, comprising the Old and New Testaments, is the Word of God, guiding people to Jesus Christ, the Redeemer. I hope the scriptures move you as they moved the two disciples whom Jesus inspired with teachings from the Old Testament. Before moving on, the group paused their travels to eat, and Jesus broke bread with the two disciples. The disciples didn't realize who he really was until Jesus broke bread with them.

> Luke 24:30-32 "When he was at table with them, he took the bread and blessed and broke it and gave it to them. 31 And their eyes were opened, and they recognized him. And he vanished from their sight. 32 They said to each other, "Did not our hearts burn within us while he talked to us on the road, while he opened to us the Scriptures?""

The scriptures concerning Jesus ignited a burning passion within their hearts. The Hebrew word translated as "burn", their hearts burned within them, also signifies "to set on fire". As we go through the scriptures, I hope your heart is set on fire, and you feel a deep passion for Christ. Despite the world's seeming indifference, the existence of God remains undeniable. While the world is unaware, God's presence is undeniable, and He continues to work. The death of Jesus on the cross was followed by his burial; the king is dead. Jesus Christ's resurrection from the tomb occurred on the third day, marking his entrance into eternal life. The King is alive again.

The King is dead, Long Live the King!

Chapter two.

Empty Pews.

Matthew 16:17-18 And Jesus answered him, "Blessed are you, Simon Bar-Jonah! For flesh and blood has not revealed this to you, but my Father who is in heaven. 18 And I tell you, you are Peter, and on this rock I will build my church, and the gates of hell shall not prevail against it."

Regrettably, over the last half-century, Church attendance has exhibited a consistent decline, particularly within Westernized nations. Church attendance in the United States, the United Kingdom, Australia, and various European nations is at an unprecedented low. A consensus amongst commentators suggests we are currently experiencing a post-Christian era. What are the primary motivations behind people's decisions to no longer participate in church activities? Does the decline in church attendance reflect a loss of faith among the populace? Could it be that they maintain their faith but make a conscious decision not to attend Church? Research indicates that individuals affiliated with a particular religious denomination may transition to another denomination. According to a study I have reviewed, there is a demonstrable growth in the number of churches that base their teachings on the Bible. Their findings indicated the opposite to be the case in institutions that promote culturally sensitive progressive teachings. We are observing an increase in the number of "house Church" groups unaffiliated with any major Christian denominations. A study conducted by the Barna Group, and released by the Baptist Church in the USA, has yielded the following findings. The Barna Group, report stated that 70 million Americans routinely participate in or have explored the concept of a house church.

According to the report, there has been an eight percent rise since 1996. They indicated that the House Church movement is exhibiting characteristics of lasting permanence. "Contemporary understandings and engagements with 'church' are undergoing a rapid transformation driven by a form of 'religious choice,' where individuals are increasingly assuming personal responsibility for their spiritual journey and growth," Barna group stated in the report. The quote concludes. Research conducted at the University of Melbourne in 2020 revealed a substantial decrease in the percentage of Australians who identified with the Christian faith, dropping from approximately 70 percent in 2004 to a mere 51 percent in 2018. Notwithstanding an increase in attendance at House Churches, official statistics indicate a decline in the number of individuals identifying as Christian. Consideration must also be given to the substantial influx of migrants from diverse religious backgrounds.

The statistics provided illuminate the substantial challenges that confronts the Church. A post-Christian society is characterized by a decline in Christianity's dominance as the primary civil religion, leading to an adoption of values, cultural practices, and perspectives that are not necessarily derived from Christian beliefs. Disclosure of multiple sexual misconduct incidents within the Church has eroded public confidence. The gradual encroachment of secular values into the Church's liturgical practices has contributed to internal divisions. Increased affluence in Western counties, surpassing previous levels, has engendered a sense of contentment, leading some to perceive a decreased need for the Church. CNN has reported that, as of present day, roughly 64% of Americans identify with the Christian faith. While this figure may seem substantial, it's worth noting that in 1970, this percentage was 90%, as per a 2020 study by the Pew Research Center. The same survey predicts that the Christian majority in the United States could be eliminated by the year 2070. While Church attendance has decreased, as documented by CNN, there has been a parallel decline in the number of individuals who adhere to the Christian Gospel. It's regrettable that the absence of Christian education has created a void in the lives of many individuals. Both men and women are exploring avenues outside traditional domains to find meaning in their existence. As a volunteer at the community care center, I interact with people from many backgrounds. Homelessness affects a segment of the population. I've noticed a growing number of people grappling with loneliness. I spoke with a woman who said she stopped attending church because the minister sexually abused her. Her faith wavered, and she questioned why God didn't shield her from the abuse. I tried to ease her pain by reminding her that God's love is always there. I stressed that there are people in the world who are harmful and abusive. No matter their claims, they are not genuine representatives of God.

Another significant decline in the Christian faith can be attributed to the acceptance of alternative beliefs. Previously, the Church held a significant position as a focal point for both religious devotion and social cohesion. This element was indispensable for a community driven by faith and a spirit of collective responsibility. Current trends demonstrate the sale of empty church structures for real estate development. The collective spirit of the community is evident in the gatherings at football games and hotels, where sport and entertainment take center stage. It's worth mentioning that faith exists outside of the realm of religion. A significant portion of the population holds faith in some entity or individual. Many individuals exhibit a substantial level of confidence, which will be further explored later in our discussion.

In Australia we have witnessed the removal of any Christian education in public schools. In the state of Victoria this removal of religious education occurred in 2016. The Age newspaper reported the following in 2025

> "Victorian schools will scrap special religious instruction
> from class time, with changes to the state's curriculum

throwing the future of the controversial program in doubt. The Andrews government has ordered that the weekly 30-minute program move to lunchtime and before and after school in 2016 to make way for new content on world histories, cultures, faiths and ethics."

Eliminating religious education for our children stems directly from the seed planted in the human psyche from the beginning. The result is a generation that lacks understanding of God's purpose for humankind. The obvious danger here is the spiritual void it generates. A nation that loses its heritage and faith is vulnerable to outside influences. In Australia and the post-Christian West, another belief system is filling this void, one that will eventually dismantle our culture and profoundly affect everyone's lives. Australian society will transform into a Middle Eastern culture resembling the third world.

It is important to acknowledge that as Western prosperity increases, leading to a higher standard of living compared to 70 years ago, there is a concurrent decline in Christian faith. As wealthier countries see a decrease in church membership, poorer nations are experiencing an unprecedented growth in the Christian faith. It's not God who has abandoned the United States, Australia, and the United Kingdom, but rather those nations that have turned away from Him. It seems that the Holy Spirit's focus has shifted to nations that are earnestly pursuing the faith of Jesus Christ. The work of God continues to be evident in the world. In Asia evidence of this can be seen in the increasing prevalence of the Christian Church, unfortunately that is not the same for the Western nations. Repeating what Jesus said,

> "I will build my church, and the gates of hell shall not prevail against it." Matthew 16:18.

The title of my upcoming book is "Where is the One True Church? It will become apparent that Jesus upheld his promise.

Chapter three.

Faith and science.

Romans 1:18-20 "For the wrath of God is revealed from heaven against all ungodliness and unrighteousness of men, who by their unrighteousness suppress the truth. 19 For what can be known about God is plain to them, because God has shown it to them. 20 For his invisible attributes his eternal power and divine nature, have been clearly perceived, ever since the creation of the world, in the things that have been made. So they are without excuse."

The sequence of scientific discoveries in the seventeenth century significantly altered the prevailing power dynamics within the Western world. The ascendancy of science as the ultimate source of knowledge has diminished the Church's authority as the preeminent institution. Scientific advancements raised questions about the credibility of Christian teachings, presenting contradictory evidence. Scientific endeavors have enabled humanity to comprehend the mechanisms of the natural world. Scientific progress paved the way for the exclusion of religious instruction in the educational setting. The influence of secular science constitutes one of the most significant threats to the Christian faith in modern times. It's important to acknowledge that scientists, too, hold faith regarding the origin of the universe. It's essential to recognize that numerous aspects of human existence transcend the scope of scientific observation and experimentation. While scientific methods like observation and experimentation are crucial for sound scientific practice, a substantial body of knowledge exists outside the scope of empirical science. Here are a few examples that science alone cannot explain. What is the fundamental reason for the existence of life? How did the universe originate from a state of non-existence?

While scientific theories abound regarding these inquiries, scientists' underlying assumptions are subject to continual revision and refinement. Astronomers have recently amended their theoretical understanding of the Universe's genesis. Scientific methods are unable to definitively explain the emergence of life from non-life. In response to inquiries concerning the origins of life, the prominent atheist Richard Dawkins offered this concise answer: "We do not know."

For numerous decades, the populace has been influenced by secular science to believe that it possesses the answers to all life's questions. Despite extensive research, the exact nature of life's emergence continues to elude scientific explanation. They hypothesize and frequently disregard data that conflicts with their theory. Secular scientific pursuits do not acknowledge the existence of God. Secular science endeavors to exclude God from the intellectual development of our youth. Contemporary education systems have resulted in generations of students who have not been exposed to traditional religious teachings. Its lack of emotion characterizes secular science. Science is typically seen as a detached and dispassionate field of study. Consequently, our children are instructed that the universe originated from nothingness, that order emerged from chaos, and that life arose from non-life. Educators have largely eliminated religious instruction from the curriculum in most educational institutions. How is it possible for a nation to pay tribute to God when His presence is so conspicuously absent in its institutions and public life? I am not criticizing science; Scientist have made enormous advances in many scientific fields. I hold scientific endeavors that rely on observation and testing in high regard. Yet, I find it problematic when scientists dismiss the possibility of a divine creator.

> 1 Corinthians 1:18-21 For the word of the cross is folly to those who are perishing, but to us who are being saved it is the power of God. 19 For it is written, "I will destroy the

wisdom of the wise, and the discernment of the discerning I will thwart." 20 Where is the one who is wise? Where is the scribe? Where is the debater of this age? Has not God made foolish the wisdom of the world? 21 For since, in the wisdom of God, the world did not know God through wisdom, it pleased God through the folly of what we preach to save those who believe.

Chapter four.

The Word.

Genesis 1:1 "In the beginning, God created the heavens and the earth."

I am disappointed to have found individuals, some of whom are Christians, attempting to integrate scientific theory and biblical interpretation. It doesn't work. Sometimes, atheists unwavering in their beliefs intensely display emotions when someone opposes their views. It's advisable to avoid debating with adversaries, since these interactions can escalate disagreements and create emotional distress. Live the life of a Christian, "always being prepared to make a defense to anyone who asks you for a reason for the hope that is in you; yet do it with gentleness and respect." 1 Peter 3:15. There is only one truth. It is inherently impossible for conflicting evidence to be simultaneously true. Contemporary discourse frequently features the assertion that "what is true for you may not be true for me." Authors Francis J. Beckwith and Gregory Koukl, in their book on relativism titled "Feet Planted Firmly In Mid-Air," wrote.

> "When truth dies, all of its subspecies, such as ethics, perish with it. If truth can't be known, then the concept of moral truth becomes incoherent. Ethics becomes relative, right and wrong matters of individual opinion. This may seem a moral liberty, but it ultimately rings hollow. "The freedom of our day," lamented a graduate in a Harvard commencement address, "is the freedom to devote ourselves to any values we please, on the mere condition that we do not believe them to be true." End quote.

Because the Bible claims to be the inerrant word of God, it must be completely true. Of course, translators don't translate some words perfectly, but the Bible's message remains intact. If any part of the scriptures is inaccurate, it forces us to examine what makes up a reliable basis for truth. Jesus, the Son of God, is authentically who he claims to be: the way, the truth, and the life; he is therefore the savior.

John 14:6 Jesus said to him, "I am the way, and the truth, and the life. No one comes to the Father except through me."

Do we believe that? Is Jesus the absolute truth? Does he speak the truth? Should you disbelieve his words, then dispose of this book, and you should do the same with your Bible. I urge you not to dismiss the word of God. Why? Because accurate knowledge comes only from Jesus Christ. There is much confusion in the world. Gender confusion arises from not believing in the teachings of God. Yet, Jesus taught us that there are only two genders.

Mark 10:6 "But from the beginning of creation, God made them male and female."

Why do some Christians stray from the teachings of Jesus? Are they afraid of being mocked for believing the biblical creation story? Many Christian educators and religious leaders have embraced the theory of evolution. The persuasive arguments and technical terminology used by some scientists have led to the silencing of certain Christian perspectives on the Genesis account. This is an example of one of the dangerous effects I mentioned earlier. The prevailing secular theory is planting a dangerous seed in the human psyche. Was Jesus mistaken when he said from the very beginning God created them male and female? Did Jesus suggest that God, the creator of time, had an inaccurate understanding of the universe's age? Did the divine creator of the universe, billions of years in the past, subsequently develop humanity from a primate ancestor within a comparatively recent period? Secular scientific consensus suggests that Homo sapiens, modern humans, have existed for approximately 40,000 years. Secular scientists posit that the universe has been in existence for 13.8 billion years. Let us engage in some mathematical calculations. Subtracting 40,000 years from the scientific estimate of 3.8 billion years for the age of the universe reveals that the universe was already 13.76 billion years old when humans first appeared. Consequently, Jesus' initial pronouncement +from the beginning" would be deemed fundamentally erroneous. Secular science would say Jesus was significantly off the mark. Regrettably, certain Christian individuals accept the findings of secular scientists who assert that humanity's existence dates back 40,000 years. Those who support this assertion, be they atheists or Christians, contradict the truth as proclaimed by Jesus. Does the phrase "from the beginning," attributed to Jesus, accurately reflect the chronology of events? If so, we can confidently assume that Jesus has a comprehensive understanding of the precise moment and method of creation.

> John 1:1 "In the beginning was the Word, and the Word was with God, and the Word was God. 2 He was in the beginning with God. 3 All things were made through him, and without him was not any thing made that was made."

It is plainly stated in scripture that the Word is the origin of everything, without exception. The stars, planets, Earth, trees, animals, and all of humanity, both male and female, were brought into existence through the Word. Therefore, what or who constitutes the word? This is the most profound and significant truth regarding Jesus.

> John 1:10-14 "He was in the world, and the world was made through him, yet the world did not know him. 11 He came to his own, and his own people did not receive him. 12 But

to all who did receive him, who believed in his name, he gave the right to become children of God, 13 who were born, not of blood nor of the will of the flesh nor of the will of man, but of God. 14 And the Word became flesh and dwelt among us, and we have seen his glory, glory as of the only Son from the Father, full of grace and truth."

Jesus was in existence with God the Father before the beginning of time. All physical creation was brought into being through Jesus, who was the word. It is thus pertinent to ask whether the creator of humanity could have misjudged the timing. The Old Testament's events are affirmed by Jesus as factual. Noah's flood, for example, continues to be met with skepticism, unfortunately even from some people within the Christian community.

> Matthew 24:36-39 "But concerning that day and hour no one knows, not even the angels of heaven, nor the Son, but the Father only. 37 For as were the days of Noah, so will be the coming of the Son of Man. 38 For as in those days before the flood they were eating and drinking, marrying and giving in marriage, until the day when Noah entered the ark, 39 and they were unaware until the flood came and swept them all away, so will be the coming of the Son of Man."

Was the account of Noah's flood presented by Jesus as a metaphorical narrative? Absolutely not. Prior to his earthly incarnation, Jesus existed as the Word with God. Jesus was the primary speaker in the Old Testament. He was the embodiment of the Logos. In the Gospel of John, it's stated that the Word is Jesus. The term "Word" is derived from the Greek word "Logos." "In the beginning, the word (Logos) was with God and was God." Logos means the spoken and written word. The term "logos" encompasses the concept of reasoning.

The English word "logic" is derived from that Greek word. It's important to note that not all scientists dismiss the narrative found in the Bible. Numerous eminent scientists have concluded that their scientific findings align with biblical accounts. Jesus affirmed the legitimacy of the Old Testament's account of Sodom and the impending judgment.

> Luke 17:28-30 "Likewise, just as it was in the days of Lot—they were eating and drinking, buying and selling, planting and building, 29 but on the day when Lot went out from Sodom, fire and sulfur rained from heaven and destroyed them all— 30 so will it be on the day when the Son of Man is revealed."

Jesus affirmed the veracity of the account of Jonah and the great fish.

> Matthew 12:39-41 But he answered them, "An evil and adulterous generation seeks for a sign, but no sign will be given to it except the sign of the prophet Jonah. 40 For just as Jonah was three days and three nights in the belly of the great fish, so will the Son of Man be three days and three nights in the heart of the earth. 41 The men of Nineveh will rise up at the judgment with this generation and condemn it, for they repented at the preaching of Jonah, and behold, something greater than Jonah is here.

There is no reason for Jesus to falsify these claims. The events mentioned by Jesus happened. Was there a specific reason for their happening, or was it purely arbitrary? No, they occurred as a testament to the coming of Christ. Jesus drew a parallel between the story of Jonah and his own impending burial, signifying its symbolic significance. The devastation wrought by the flood and the fiery destruction of Sodom serve as cautionary tales for contemporary society. They foreshadow what is yet to be; future. It's imperative that we acknowledge the literal nature of these warnings and refrain from dismissing them. The secular and hostile environment of the present day poses a significant challenge to the upbringing of future generations. The fundamental truth found in Genesis chapter one is crucial to Christian teaching, as a lack of its instruction could allow for misinterpretation of the Bible by those who seek to promote alternative doctrines. That statement holds significant weight. Certain contemporary entities are actively engaged in revising the sacred text of the Bible. Since the dawn of time, Satan has been actively sowing seeds of doubt among the people of the world.

Before proceeding, have you ever calculated the number of years that elapsed between Adam and Jesus? Biblical accounts document the chronological and genealogical lineage. Any individual can calculate that the cumulative lifespan of the patriarchs from Adam to Jesus is roughly 4000 years. Jesus declared that the creation of Adam and Eve took place in the beginning, not 40,000 years ago. It's generally accepted that the birth of Jesus occurred approximately two millennia ago. Therefore, we can estimate the age of humanity to be approximately 6,000 years. We are presented with a choice; do we believe God's word, or man's theory?

> Proverbs 21:28 "A false witness will perish, but the word of a man who hears will endure."

Chapter Five.

Holy be thy Name.

22

Psalm 135:13 "Your name, O LORD, endures forever, your renown, O LORD, throughout all ages."

The disciples posed a question to Jesus regarding the appropriate method for addressing God in prayer. The paramount theme of this prayer, and indeed of our lives, should be the acknowledgment of God's sovereignty. His glory deserves our utmost respect and awe.

Matthew 6:9 "Pray then like this: Our Father in heaven, hallowed be your name."

This was and is a profound revelation. The almighty God wants us to call him our Father. This directive from Jesus significantly impacts our view of life and transforms how we perceive the Almighty God. Are we truly cognizant of the significance of Jesus' actions? Prior to the advent of Jesus, humankind had become estranged from God. It was impossible for anyone deemed a sinner to come before God and remain alive. When God came down on the mountain to speak to the Israelites, they were told, "do not come near the mountain." Washing their clothes and observing a spatial distance from God were necessary, while they were to remain silent and attentive.

Exodus 19:10-13 the LORD said to Moses, "Go to the people and consecrate them today and tomorrow, and let them wash their garments 11 and be ready for the third day. For on the third day the LORD will come down on Mount Sinai in the sight of all the people. 12 And you shall set limits for the people all around, saying, 'Take care not to go up into the mountain or touch the edge of it. Whoever touches the mountain shall be put to death. 13 No hand shall touch him, but he shall be stoned or shot; whether beast or man, he shall not live.' When the trumpet sounds a long blast, they shall come up to the mountain."

The advent of Jesus ushered in a transformative shift in the divine relationship with mankind. Through the blood of Jesus, we have been cleansed and are now able to approach God with confidence. By virtue of Jesus, God is now known to us as our Father. We are His children. It's imperative that we recognize His name as sacred. The Father possesses ultimate authority. To fear God is to recognize and honor the sanctity of His name with the utmost respect. This is the foundation of wisdom.

Proverbs 9:10 "The fear of the LORD is the beginning of wisdom, and the knowledge of the Holy One is insight."

Those who choose to reject the word of God show disrespect for His name. Those who venerate the created, instead of the creator, disrespect His name. The desecration of God's name could potentially result in the replacement of God with another god. That is an unavoidable outcome. Further discourse on that specific topic will be provided later in the book. It's essential that we experience God's presence in our lives. My point is that we must actively cultivate our relationship with Him daily, as faith in His word initiates a transformation. As we delve into God's Word, I pray that you will be blessed with the grace of God to broaden your comprehension of the transformation. The name of God is deemed as holy. The definition of the word "Holy"? The term "holy" is derived from the Hebrew word "qâdash," which signifies "to be set apart, to be perfect, and free from impurity."

We ought to treat God's name with the utmost respect. The Hebrew term "qâdash," which translates to "Holy," is prominent in the first book of the Bible.

> Genesis 2:1-3 "Thus the heavens and the earth were finished, and all the host of them. 2 And on the seventh day God finished his work that he had done, and he rested on the seventh day from all his work that he had done. 3 So God blessed the seventh day and made it holy (qâdash), because on it God rested from all his work that he had done in creation."

In the act of creation, God set apart the seventh day, imbuing it with divine favor and declaring it holy, distinct from the preceding days. Some maintain that the divine consecration of this day was in foresight of mankind's eventual development of the theory of evolution. When we disregard or discount the biblical account of creation, including the Sabbath, we effectively repudiate the Word of God. Humans have established an explanation for the origins of the universe that excludes the concept of God. The ancient Israelites were instructed to observe that day as holy. Why? to remind them of the divine nature of God, the Creator. The Sabbath serves as a remembrance of the divine Creator, whose watchful care over His people resembles a father's love for his children.

> Exodus 20:8-11 "Remember the Sabbath day, to keep it holy. 9 Six days you shall labor, and do all your work, 10 but the seventh day is a Sabbath to the LORD your God. On it you shall not do any work, you, or your son, or your daughter, your male servant, or your female servant, or your livestock, or the sojourner who is within your gates."

What was the divine motivation behind God's command to the Israelites? Was God's intention to establish a challenging existence, providing a reason for subsequent divine retribution? Absolutely not. This group of people practiced pagan idolatry in ancient Egypt. God intended for them to acknowledge His authority as the sole Creator. The following verse presents God's explanation to the people regarding the significance of remembering the seventh day.

Exodus 20:11 For in six days the LORD made heaven and earth, the sea, and all that is in them, and rested on the seventh day. Therefore, the LORD blessed the Sabbath day and made it holy."

It's a privilege for those who recognize the Sabbath as a divine gift, a reminder of God the Creator's fatherly role in our lives and the sanctity of His name. In the New Testament, the word "Holy" is derived from the Koine Greek word "hagiazo."

(ISV). Luke 11:2 So he told them, "Whenever you pray you are to say, 'Father, may we may keep your name holy (hagiazo). May your kingdom come."

Both the Greek term "hagiazo" and the Hebrew term "qâdash" share the same meaning. God's sacred calling of "holy" encompasses all that He reserves for Himself, which includes you.

1 Peter 1:14-16 As obedient children, do not be conformed to the passions of your former ignorance, 15 but as he who called you is holy, you also be holy in all your conduct, 16 since it is written, "You shall be holy, for I am holy."

Chapter Six.

Our Father.

Deuteronomy 3:24 "O Lord GOD, you have only begun to show your servant your greatness and your mighty hand. For what god is there in heaven or on earth who can do such works and mighty acts as yours?"

God's divine name holds profound significance, as it not only underscores the greatness but also unveils God's intrinsic nature and character. Here's a sample from my previous work, without repeating the entire text. The name "Yahveh," occasionally rendered as "Yahweh," is the revered and holy designation for God in the Hebrew language. Some argue the name should be translated as Jehovah, but as the letter J is not in the Hebrew language, that interpretation should be Yehovah. Jewish scholars have identified a range of meanings associated with the Hebrew name for God. The Tetragrammaton is the combination of four Hebrew letters to form the ancient Hebrew name of God, YHWH. The suggested interpretation of the name is "to Be," meaning an eternal presence (omnipresence). Moreover, certain scholars propose that the name signifies "the one who brings forth all existence." Also, "I will be with you."

At the age of 30 when Jesus began his ministry, he introduced God as our Father. As recorded in Luke 11:2, Jesus provided a model prayer, instructing his followers to begin with the words, "Father, hallowed be your name." Jesus told us to call God "Father," translated from the Greek word Pater, which literally means Father. This information has significant implications for our situation. How? The divine essence, the origin of all creation, the all-powerful God, is no longer remote from us. The notion of God being situated in a remote, celestial location is now obsolete. We have now been united to God as his family. This relationship is distinct and contrasts with all other religious affiliations. God is our Father. According to Jewish and Islamic tenets, this announcement constitutes blasphemy; however, this is what God ordained prior to creation.

> Genesis 1:27 So God created man in his own image, in the image of God he created him; male and female he created them.

During the era of Jesus, prominent religious groups included the Pharisees, the Sadducees, and the Essenes. Despite their shared Jewish heritage, these groups held divergent interpretations of the Torah. The Pharisees held the most significant position among the three groups, as they are considered the spiritual progenitors of contemporary Judaism. Their primary defining attribute was the belief in an Oral Law, which they maintained was divinely revealed to Moses at Mount Sinai alongside the written Torah. The Pharisees espoused the belief in the resurrection of the dead, encompassing the concept of an afterlife. Conversely, the Sadducees held beliefs that contradicted both ideas. The Pharisees held the belief in the existence of a spiritual realm inhabited by angels. The Sadducees maintained a position of social elitism, separating themselves from the general populace. Their objective was to preserve the priestly class. The Sadducees, unlike the Pharisees, embraced Hellenistic influences in their daily lives. The Sadducees, in contrast to other Jewish sects, disregarded the Oral Law and strictly adhered to a literal reading of the Written Law. Sadducee life centered on rituals related to the Temple. The Essenes, a third faction, emerged because of their disdain for the other two. This sect maintained that the others had corrupted the city of Jerusalem, and the Temple. They relocated from Jerusalem to live a monastic life in the desert, adopting rigorous dietary regulations and embracing celibacy. Jesus encountered individuals who were legalistically inclined, frequently rebuking them for their hypocrisy. Jesus was accused of blasphemy by the religious leaders of his time for claiming God as his Father.

Ultimately, Jesus faced accusations and arrest at the hands of the Jewish leadership. Jesus was brought before the Roman governor Pontius Pilate, who, finding no fault in him, sought to release him. However, the Jewish leaders demanded Jesus' crucifixion. Subsequent verses detail the specific accusations levied against Jesus by Jewish authorities.

> John 19:5-7 "So Jesus came out, wearing the crown of thorns and the purple robe. Pilate said to them, "Behold the man!" 6 When the chief priests and the officers saw him, they cried out, "Crucify him, crucify him!" Pilate said to them, "Take him yourselves and crucify him, for I find no guilt in him." 7 The Jews answered him, "We have a law, and according to that law he ought to die because he has made himself the Son of God."

The accusation against Jesus stemmed from his assertion of being the Son of God. How many individuals are aware of the pre-existence of Jesus as God, prior to his earthly incarnation as the "son of God." All four Gospels document that Jesus referred to God as his Father. Jesus taught that we should refer to God as our Father. Does this qualify us as children of God? Within the Jewish tradition and the Islamic faith, using the term "Father" to refer to God would also be considered blasphemous. Why would that be considered sacrilege from the perspective of these monotheistic religions? Both religions assert the monotheistic principle of God's singularity and deny the existence of a divine son. Consequently, anyone claiming to be a son of God, within the framework of these beliefs, is seen as elevating themselves to the status of divinity. Such an act was deemed sacrilegious, punishable by death.

John 5:18 "This was why the Jews were seeking all the more to kill him, because not only was he breaking the Sabbath, but he was even calling God his own Father, making himself equal with God."

The opening verses of the Gospel of John reveal the identity of the Word of God. We previously read, John asserts that the Word became incarnate, and subsequently, he posits that those who believe in him are considered "children of God."

John 1:10-13 "He was in the world, and the world was made through him, yet the world did not know him. 11 He came to his own, and his own people did not receive him. 12 But to all who did receive him, who believed in his name, he gave the right to become children of God, 13 who were born, not of blood nor of the will of the flesh nor of the will of man, but of God."

Those who exercise faith have been granted the status of God's children, now addressing God as Father. The revelation of Jesus Christ unveils the profound mystery of God expanding His family. While the child cannot become the parent, we are invited to emulate His nature, cultivating a heart and love akin to His own.

Ephesians 1:3-6 "Blessed be the God and Father of our Lord Jesus Christ, who has blessed us in Christ with every spiritual blessing in the heavenly places, 4 even as he chose us in him before the foundation of the world, that we should be holy and blameless before him. In love 5 he predestined us for adoption to himself as sons through Jesus Christ, according to the purpose of his will, 6 to the praise of his glorious grace, with which he has blessed us in the Beloved."

Chapter seven.

Child of God.

In the evening preceding the commencement of this chapter, I engaged in a conversation with a young man regarding the existence of God. This is not the first occasion I have engaged in a discussion about the existence of God. This young man, and many individuals struggle to reconcile the presence of suffering and evil in the world with the concept there is an all-powerful, all-loving deity. Convincing those who reject the message of Jesus, our redeemer, proves to be a difficult endeavor. I have chosen titles for the next five chapters, each commencing with the letter "A." These five words, all starting with "A," constitute a transgression against the divine and represent a rejection of God's presence. The five A words serve as metaphorical blindfolds, obscuring the potential for individuals to experience the profound gift of being adopted into God's family. I wish to refocus attention on the concept of God's family, the children of God, in the context of the end times. We are now in the last days. This period signifies the immediate prelude to the tribulation and the advent of Jesus Christ, the King, who will establish the Kingdom of God on Earth. Numerous scriptural passages predict the occurrence of an end time, also referred to as the last days.

> Hebrews 1:1-2 "Long ago, at many times and God spoke to our fathers by the prophets, 2 but in these last days he has spoken to us by his Son, whom he appointed the heir of all things, through whom also he created the world."

It's amazing that God created all things through the Word, and the Word came in human form; Jesus, who is the Son of God. Jesus, who was one with God and possessed the divine essence, came into this physical world. As a man, he entered the reality that he had brought into existence. In accordance with the Christian faith, Jesus Christ embodied human form, experiencing life as one of us, and is now designated as heir to all creation. Read John 1:1-14. Jesus, the firstborn son of God was resurrected from death to life, yet his existence predates time, having been with God from the beginning, in the spirit. The apostle Paul eloquently articulated this truth in his epistle to the Colossian church.

Colossians 1:15-18 "He is the image of the invisible God, the firstborn of all creation. 16 For by him all things were created, in heaven and on earth, visible and invisible, whether thrones or dominions or rulers or authorities—all things were created through him and for him. 17 And he is before all things, and in him all things hold together. 18 And he is the head of the body, the church. He is the beginning, the firstborn from the dead, that in everything he might be preeminent."

Jesus Christ's arrival was intended to bring humanity back to God, atoning for their transgressions through his own sacrifice. As the first born from the dead, he paves the way for others to will follow and receiving immortality. Paul asserts that believers will undergo a transformation, wherein our mortal bodies will become immortal. Paul the Apostle extended words of encouragement to the church in Corinth, as he did to all churches.

1 Corinthians 15:51-57 "Behold! I tell you a mystery. We shall not all sleep, but we shall all be changed, 52 in a moment, in the twinkling of an eye, at the last trumpet. For the trumpet will sound, and the dead will be raised

imperishable, and we shall be changed. 53 For this perishable body must put on the imperishable, and this mortal body must put on immortality. 54 When the perishable puts on the imperishable, and the mortal puts on immortality, then shall come to pass the saying that is written: "Death is swallowed up in victory." 55 "O death, where is your victory? O death, where is your sting?" 56 The sting of death is sin, and the power of sin is the law. 57 But thanks be to God, who gives us the victory through our Lord Jesus Christ."

This news holds significant importance for all individuals. This constitutes the core message of the Gospel. Jesus paved the way for all to follow. His resurrection, a victory over death, paves the way for us to follow him into paradise. By virtue of our human existence, we are all children of God. We are privileged to live in these latter days, and there are many reasons to rejoice. Approximately two millennia ago, Jesus Christ arrived to liberate humanity from the power of death, atoning for our transgressions, thereby enabling us to experience renewed life. It's a foundational belief in Christianity that Jesus is the Son of God. The disciples witnessed Jesus' transfiguration, an event that revealed his true divine identity. The reliable witnesses fortunately shared the truth in the Gospels.

Luke 9:28-35 "Now about eight days after these sayings he took with him Peter and John and James and went up on the mountain to pray. 29 And as he was praying, the appearance of his face was altered, and his clothing became dazzling white. 30 And behold, two men were talking with him, Moses and Elijah, 31 who appeared in glory and spoke of his departure, which he was about to accomplish at Jerusalem. 32 Now Peter and those who were with him were heavy with sleep, but when they became fully awake they saw his glory and the two men who stood with him. 33 And as the men were parting from him, Peter said to Jesus, "Master, it is good that we are here. Let us make three tents, one for you and one for Moses and one for Elijah"—not knowing what he said. 34 As he was saying these things, a cloud came and overshadowed them, and they were afraid as they entered the cloud. 35 And a voice came out of the cloud, saying, "This is my Son, my Chosen One; listen to him!"

Christian theology teaches that Jesus is the firstborn son of God. Jesus, in response to the question of prayer, showed us not only how to pray but also the one to whom we should pray; Luke 11:2. The appropriate term of address for God is "Father." How do we honour God as Father? In what ways can a child demonstrate respect and honor towards their parents? Let us not forget the fifth commandment, which calls for the honoring of our parents. The importance of this matter is evident in its high position on the 10 commandments. If we cannot demonstrate reverence for our earthly parents, how can we expect to show true devotion to God? Our innate nature inclines us towards the establishment of positive and safe relationships, ideally within the framework of a family. Engaging in familial bonding cultivates a deeper relationship with the divine Creator. The Hebrew term translated as "honor" is "kabad."

> Leviticus 19:3 "Every one of you shall revere his mother and his father, and you shall keep my Sabbaths: I am the LORD your God."

From the outset, God's divine plan involved both male and female, husband and wife, as the foundation for procreation, family building, and the development of familial bonds. These gifts from God to humanity deserve respectful treatment and should not be misused. The earthly family serves as a reflection of the divine family.

Genesis 1:27-28 So God created man in his own image, in the image of God he created him; male and female he created them. 28 And God blessed them. And God said to them, "Be fruitful and multiply and fill the earth and subdue it, and have dominion over the fish of the sea and over the birds of the heavens and over every living thing that moves on the earth."

God is the supreme being of order, not of disorder. The universe bears testament to the beauty and order inherent in God's creation. The delicate equilibrium of life on Earth is fundamental to its existence. We are consequently obligated to revere, honor, and respect God as our Father. The question is. how can we prevent God from being God? The following five chapters will delve into my selection of five A words. The five A words represent facets of human nature, emanating from a primal instinct inherent within every individual. They impede the understanding of God's truth. Their presence constitutes a flaw in human character, a flaw that has the potential to undermine humanity.

Romans 5:6 "For while we were still weak, at the right time Christ died for the ungodly."

Jesus came to pave the way for all to follow him, paying the penalty for our sins. He is the head, the first of many to be resurrected to immortal life. Paul discloses that a transformation awaits us, as our mortal body will assume immortality. Paul the Apostle offered encouragement to the church in Corinth, as he did with all the Churches. In a previous section we read the encouragement offered by Paul to the Church in Corinth. 1 Corinthians 15:51-57

This is the most important news for all people. This is the Gospel message. Jesus paved the way. He defeated death in his resurrection, so that we could follow. We are all born children of God in the flesh; yet we must be born again to be adopted children of God, born in the Spirit.

> 1 Peter 1:3-5 "Blessed be the God and Father of our Lord Jesus Christ! According to his great mercy, he has caused us to be born again to a living hope through the resurrection of Jesus Christ from the dead, 4 to an inheritance that is imperishable, undefiled, and unfading, kept in heaven for you, 5 who by God's power are being guarded through faith for a salvation ready to be revealed in the last time."

It's a blessing for all of us to be living in these last days, why? Around 2000 years ago, Jesus came to deliver us from death, to pay the penalty for our sins, so that we may have life in the Spirit. Jesus is the son of God; the Bible makes that very clear. Jesus was transfigured on the mount, so that his disciples could witness and record for us today a revelation confirming the eminence of Jesus.

> Luke 9: 35 And a voice came out of the cloud, saying, "This is my Son, my Chosen One; listen to him!"

Jesus is the firstborn son of God; he paved the way for us to follow. When asked how we should pray, Jesus said; "When you pray, say: "Father, hallowed be your name. Your kingdom come." Luke 11:2. We are to call God "Father." If God (Yahveh) is our Father, we are surely His children. How do we honour God as Father? How does a child honour their father and mother? Remember the 5th commandment, to honour our parents. This is so important God placed the command very high on the list, right in the middle. If we cannot honour our earthly parents, how are we going to honour God? We are born for relationships, to have good, safe relationships within a family environment. Unfortunately many families are divided in our post-Christian society. Engaging in family bonding enables us to center our attention on our relationship with the divine Creator. The Hebrew word translated honour is "kâbad." The word means heavy, not heavy-handed, but to revere your parents, to respect them.

> Leviticus 19:3 "Every one of you shall revere his mother and his father, and you shall keep my Sabbaths: I am the LORD your God."

From the very beginning, God intended male and female, husband and wife, to have children, build families and forming family relationships. These are blessings from God to humanity; they should not be abused. The physical family unit mirrors the Spiritual God family. We have read this from the account of creation week.

> Genesis 1:8 So God created man in his own image, in the image of God he created him; male and female he created them.

God is the God of order, not chaos. The universe is witness to God's beauty and order. Life on Earth is underpinned by a finely-tuned balance. So we are to honour, respect and revere God as our Father. The question is, how can we stop God being God? In the following five chapters, we will cover the five A words. The five A words are branches growing out of *that seed* of thought planted within every human psyche. They are a barrier to God's truth. They are the downfall of humanity, a flaw of character.

Romans 5:6 "For while we were still weak, at the right time Christ died for the ungodly."

The following five chapters begin with letters describing the human dilemma.

Chapter eight.

A is for Apathy.

Jeremiah 22:21 "I spoke to you in your prosperity, but you said, 'I will not listen.' This has been your way from your youth, that you have not obeyed my voice."

Our first term, laden with negativity, is apathy. It's important to recognize that apathy or indifference does not signify a total absence of concern. Apathetic people are typically occupied with their own activities. Those who display indifference to the concept of God tend to lead very busy lives. They occupy their lives with a variety of responsibilities, as well as pursuits for entertainment and pleasure, unburdened by worry. Preceding my acceptance of faith, I was heavily engaged in playing sports, managing teams, and working for a living. My time was fully occupied, leaving little opportunity for other activities. There was no leisure time dedicated to spiritual devotion. I concluded that a relationship with God was not a pressing concern, as its relevance to my current life was minimal. If we prioritize worldly matters over spiritual ones, we will be less receptive to the Gospel's message, resulting in indifference. The Cambridge Dictionary defines apathy as follows:

"A behaviour that shows no interest or energy and shows that someone is unwilling to take action, especially over something important."

While we may demonstrate considerable zeal in our personal lives, our attitude towards God is often characterized by indifference. The apathy that characterizes our relationship with God, though profoundly grave, is often overlooked. Apathy towards God is the primary source of the most serious repercussions. One of the most formidable challenges to the propagation of the Gospel message is overcoming the barrier of apathy. Everyone possesses individual preferences. Our interests are selective, with some subjects holding our attention while others fail to elicit any engagement. Ignoring God's message will ultimately result in our own downfall. We must treat God's word with the utmost seriousness. Jesus gave strict warnings regarding this form of apathy. He prophesied that before his return; humanity would be too engrossed in their lives to consider God. People will be preoccupied with personal matters during the end times. In Luke, we see the gravity of Jesus' warnings.

> Luke 17:26-30 "Just as it was in the days of Noah, so will it be in the days of the Son of Man. 27 They were eating and drinking and marrying and being given in marriage, until the day when Noah entered the ark, and the flood came and destroyed them all. 28 Likewise, just as it was in the days of Lot—they were eating and drinking, buying and selling, planting and building, 29 but on the day when Lot went out from Sodom, fire and sulfur rained from heaven and destroyed them all — 30 so will it be on the day when the Son of Man is revealed."

Jesus spoke plainly; Let's put this into modern day slang - "you people are so full of yourselves, so preoccupied with entertainment, you don't see the big truck about to run you over." Jesus is shouting "WAKE UP! The world is on the cusp of a significant change, and this transformation will occur soon. It's time for all to consider the teachings of Jesus Christ; embrace them and live, or disregard them and face the consequences. It's a certainty that death brings an end to all earthly pursuits, including sports, celebrations, and enjoyment. My previous perspective on God's word was one of indifference. Yet, following my conversion and belief in His son, I discovered that my social life remained uncompromised. My life, in fact, possessed genuine meaning, was considerably more fulfilling, and was guided by a clear purpose. I am now primarily focused on my heavenly Father and His son. The interpretation of Jesus' words regarding the world's condition during Noah's flood remains a subject of ongoing debate and diverse perspectives. While numerous individuals perceive Jesus' teachings as a condemnation of a sinful world, his message extends beyond the confines of sin. His words depicted a world marked by apathy toward both God and His divine word. This illustrates the comparison between the two ages. As with the generation before the flood, individuals will disregard the admonitions and authority of the divine. Such warnings are found throughout Scripture, including the New Testament.

2 Peter 3:3-7 "knowing this first, that scoffers will come in the last days with scoffing, following their own sinful desires. 4 They will say, "Where is the promise of his coming? For ever since the fathers fell asleep, all things are continuing as they were from the beginning of creation." 5 For they deliberately overlook this fact, that the heavens existed long ago, and the earth was formed out of water and through water by the word of God, 6 and that by means of these the world that then existed was deluged with water and perished. 7 But by the same word the heavens and earth that now exist are stored up for fire, being kept until the day of judgment and destruction of the ungodly."

In the modern era, marked by a secularization of values, the figure who died to enable a relationship with our heavenly Father is often met with indifference. Individuals are preoccupied and unable to focus on the ominous future. The words of Jesus serve as a cautionary message that we should all heed. Two distinct choices present themselves to us, each with a profound consequence: one offers life and joy, the other leads to death. Repeating an earlier verse,

Deuteronomy 30:19 "I call heaven and earth to witness against you today, that I have set before you life and death, blessing and curse. Therefore choose life, that you and your offspring may live."

Chapter nine.

A is for Anger.

Romans 14:17-19 "For the kingdom of God is not a matter of eating and drinking but of righteousness and peace and joy in the Holy Spirit. 18 Whoever thus serves Christ is acceptable to God and approved by men. 19 So then let us pursue what makes for peace and for mutual upbuilding."

The second A word is "anger." An unprecedented outpouring of anger is observable globally today. Protests characterized by violence, violent criminal activity, agitated motorists, and indignant shoppers. Today, we should anticipate encountering some anger, wherever our journey may take us. Unresolved anger can have detrimental effects on both mental and physical well-being. Anger impairs moral judgment. Individuals experiencing anger are often perpetrators of violent crimes, including mass shootings in the United States. A plethora of publications address the topics of anger and anger management. This book explores the concept of anger directed towards God. I have encountered numerous individuals who harbor resentment towards God due to the presence of evil in the world. What is the reason God allows evil and suffering to continue? Failure to understand the reason behind today's evil incites feelings of resentment towards God. It's the viewpoint of many people, if there is a God then he ought to intercede and bring an end to all violence. The young man I spoke of earlier expressed his disapproval of a God who allows children to die of cancer. He said he was shaking his fist at God, if God was there. Many people, including the young man, don't reflect on God's gracious gift of freedom. The suffering we see is often a result of the choices people make. The young man was deeply upset and let down by God, given the widespread child abuse in the world. Why does God allow some children to die without intervening? I asked him, "What proof do you have that God didn't choose to save some of these children?" There's no way to know the additional suffering a child or anyone would endure if someone were to intervene in just one case. If God did intervene, then he would need to intervene in all subsequent troubles. To eliminate evil and oppression, God would have to strip us of our free will and turn us into automatons. That would eradicate evil, but what would be the fate of love? It's impossible to compel individuals to experience love. I cannot envision my spouse consenting to having a keyboard placed on her forehead, allowing me to trigger a "kiss me" command at will. It's of paramount importance that we retain the liberty to make our own choices, and avoid attributing blame to a higher power for our shortcomings. Here's an example, closer to home. Having cautioned our son about the dangers of speeding, he disregarded our warnings, which led to the destruction of his vehicle. What would our emotional response be if he accused us of failing to remove the car from his possession?

God sent his Son, Jesus, into the world to redeem humanity from the consequences of sin, not to infringe upon human freedom. God is a just God, and will not allow evil to continue. The way out calls for repentance and accepting the forgiveness of the son of God. Our actions have resulted in environmental degradation, and we have failed to provide adequate support for vulnerable populations, including the impoverished, the sick, the elderly, and children. More importantly, the vast majority have disregarded God's son, the redeemer of humanity. I find myself angered by the current state of society, but my anger is directed at the evils that plague it, never at God. The experience of bitterness and pain is a common consequence of anger directed towards others. Forgiveness serves as a balm for the wounded soul. This does not imply acceptance of malevolent or spiteful actions. Blaming God for all the evils of the world will estrange us from His benevolent embrace. From the very beginning in the Garden of Eden, evil and anger have been present, their influence prevailing until the arrival of Jesus, the savior.

Ephesians 4:26-27 "Be angry and do not sin; do not let the sun go down on your anger, 27 and give no opportunity to the devil."

Chapter ten.

A is for Arrogance.

Psalm 73:6-7 "Therefore pride is their necklace; violence covers them as a garment. 7

Their eyes swell out through fatness; their hearts overflow with follies."

Arrogance or pride constitutes a significant obstacle to our connection with God. Remember, it is not God who distances Himself from us, but rather we who distance ourselves from Him. How is that possible? Through the manifestation of our attitude. An inflated ego is a consequence of pride. It skews and dramatically exaggerates our assessment of ourselves. Scripture offers a comprehensive perspective on the detrimental nature of pride. The act of elevating one's own righteousness inevitably results in the familiar countenance of arrogance. A sense of pride often leads individuals to view themselves as self-contained entities, not requiring assistance from others due to their perceived superiority. According to the Psalmist, those individuals demonstrably believe they have no need of God.

Psalm 10:4 "In the pride of his face the wicked does not seek him; all his thoughts are, "There is no God.""

The Collins dictionary defines - Arrogance -

"Someone who is arrogant behaves in a proud, unpleasant way towards other people because they believe that they are more important than others."

I'd like to add, even more important than God. Arrogance often manifests in a resistance to God, as individuals with such a disposition perceive themselves as more knowledgeable and capable than even the Almighty. The books of Ezekiel and Isaiah contain revelations concerning the downfall of Satan, with which you may be familiar. There is agreement among theologians that this depiction represents Satan in his pre-fallen state. The scriptures of the Old Testament frequently establish parallels between earthly kings or rulers and spiritual entities. The passages from Ezekiel demonstrate this point. The comparison between Satan and the king of Tyre focuses primarily on the characteristics of Satan. Satan, like the angels, was a created spiritual entity. He was a being of extraordinary magnificence, divinely created.

Ezekiel 28:11-19 Moreover, the word of the LORD came to me: 12 "Son of man, raise a lamentation over the king of Tyre, and say to him, Thus says the Lord GOD: "You were the signet of perfection, full of wisdom and perfect in beauty. 13 You were in Eden, the garden of God; every precious stone was your covering, sardius, topaz, and diamond, beryl, onyx, and jasper, sapphire, emerald, and carbuncle; and crafted in gold were your settings and your engravings. On the day that you were created they were prepared. 14 You were an anointed guardian cherub. I placed you; you were on the holy mountain of God; in the midst of the stones of fire you walked. 15 You were blameless in your ways from the day you were created, till unrighteousness was found in you. 16 In the abundance of your trade you were filled with violence in your midst, and you sinned; so I cast you as a profane thing from the mountain of God, and I destroyed you, O guardian cherub, from the midst of the stones of fire. 17 Your heart was proud because of your beauty; you corrupted your wisdom for the sake of your splendor. I cast you to the ground; I exposed you before kings, to feast their eyes on you. 18 By the multitude of your iniquities, in the unrighteousness of your trade you profaned your sanctuaries; so I brought fire out from your midst; it consumed you, and I turned you to ashes on the earth in the sight of all who saw you. 19 All who know you among the peoples are appalled at you; you have come to a dreadful end and shall be no more forever."

The Bible recounts that God originally created Satan as a beautiful cherub, an angel adorned with wings. Cherubim hold a significant position within the Angelic hierarchy. Divine instruction directed Moses to fashion two cherubic effigies, entrusted with the critical task of safeguarding the Ark of the Covenant.

1 Kings 8:6-7 "Then the priests brought the ark of the covenant of the LORD to its place in the inner sanctuary of the house, in the Most Holy Place, underneath the wings of the cherubim. 7 For the cherubim spread out their wings over the place of the ark, so that the cherubim overshadowed the ark and its poles."

Satan's pride was fueled by his exceptional beauty and elevated rank among the angels.

His arrogant nature resulted in wickedness. Pride can have such an influence on a person's behavior. Consequently, they seek to place themselves above others, as evidenced by the following passages. This is precisely what transpired in the case of Satan.

Isaiah 14:11-15 Your pomp (pride) is brought down to Sheol, the sound of your harps; maggots are laid as a bed beneath you, and worms are your covers. 12 "How you are fallen from heaven, O Day Star, son of Dawn! How you are cut down to the ground, you who laid the nations low! 13 You said in your heart, 'I will ascend to heaven; above the stars of God I will set my throne on high; I will sit on the mount of assembly in the far reaches of the north; 14 I will ascend above the heights of the clouds; I will make myself like the Most High.' 15 But you are brought down to Sheol, to the far reaches of the pit.

Satan's excessive pride led him to believe he could elevate himself to the level of the
Almighty. Indeed, unchecked pride can lead individuals to perceive themselves as equals to God. God alone is supreme, and He extends His favor to those who esteem Him, but He stands opposed to the proud.

Psalm 31:23 "Love the LORD, all you his saints! The LORD preserves the faithful but abundantly repays the one who acts in pride."

The scriptures contain extensive warnings about pride, emphasizing the grave consequences of this dangerous disposition. Pride, like all other human emotions, is capable of being overcome.

Proverbs 8:13 "The fear of the LORD is hatred of evil. Pride and arrogance and the way of evil and perverted speech I hate."

The vices of pride or arrogance can induce a person to engage in evil actions and speak in a distorted manner. This is crucial to comprehend, as Jesus emphasized that our words reveal the state of our hearts; in other words, our speech reflects our true nature.

Mark 7:20-23 And he said, "What comes out of a person is what defiles him. 21 For from within, out of the heart of man, come evil thoughts, sexual immorality, theft, murder, adultery, 22 coveting, wickedness, deceit, sensuality, envy, slander, pride, foolishness. 23 All these evil things come from within, and they defile a person."

Jesus explicitly categorized pride as an evil attribute within the human character. Arrogance constitutes a barrier to divine love. How, then, might we address feelings of pride? The fostering of humility is essential. Such accomplishment is brought about by the Holy Spirit, who is given to all who have faith.

Proverbs 11:2 "When pride comes, then comes disgrace, but with the humble is wisdom."

Humility before God leads to the acquisition of wisdom. How does one define humility?

What steps are necessary to reach this desired mental condition?

Proverbs 29:23 "One's pride will bring him low, but he who is lowly in spirit will obtain honor."

According to Solomon, God grants honor to those who are humble in spirit. This message emphasizes the importance of humility for Christians. Divine favor is bestowed upon those who renounce self-righteousness, an outcome of unwarranted pride. In our contemporary, secular society, the absence of a unifying religious belief poses a significant challenge. There is a pervasive sense of self-righteousness in modern society. Politicians, actors, and musicians frequently engage in public displays of moral superiority.

James 4:4 You adulterous people! Do you not know that friendship with the world is enmity with God? Therefore whoever wishes to be a friend of the world makes himself an enemy of God. 5 Or do you suppose it is to no purpose that the Scripture says, "He yearns jealously over the spirit that he has made to dwell in us"? 6 But he gives more grace. Therefore it says, "God opposes the proud but gives grace to the humble." 7 Submit yourselves therefore to God. Resist the devil, and he will flee from you."

The three "A" words we have swiftly reviewed can elicit feelings of resentment and bitterness. Individuals may experience anger towards God due to a perception that He is responsible for their misfortunes. Individuals may harbor resentment towards religious institutions and practices, perceiving them as indicative of divine wrath. Anger often leads to significant emotional distress, and the individual experiencing anger is typically the one who bears the most suffering.

James 1:19-20 "Know this, my beloved brothers: let every person be quick to hear, slow to speak, slow to anger; 20 for the anger of man does not produce the righteousness of God."

Chapter eleven.

A is for Anchored.

Hebrews 12:1-2 "Therefore, since we are surrounded by so great a cloud of witnesses, let us also lay aside every weight, and sin which clings so closely, and let us run with endurance the race that is set before us, 2 looking to Jesus, the founder and perfecter of our faith, who for the joy that was set before him endured the cross, despising the shame, and is seated at the right hand of the throne of God."

Our fourth A word, "anchored." Sin carries an unbearable weight. It hinders our capacity to fully experience the tranquility and happiness found in our faith in Jesus. Sacred texts consistently urge us to cast aside any sin that entangles us. Continued engagement in sin results in a severance or disruption of our relationship with God, and many times with other people. When we repent and receive God's Holy Spirit, we have a heightened desire to resist sin.

Romans 6:1-4 "What shall we say then? Are we to continue in sin that grace may abound? 2 Not! How can we who died to sin still live in it? 3 Do you not know that all of us who have been baptized into Christ Jesus were baptized into his death? 4 We were buried therefore with him by baptism into death, in order that, just as Christ was raised from the dead by the glory of the Father, we too might walk in newness of life."

Sin acts as a weighty anchor, hindering spiritual progress. Scripture affirms that Jesus Christ approached humanity while we were still in a state of sin, not to endorse our sinful nature, but to liberate us from its consequences. All sin is inherently harmful. It has a detrimental effect on our relationship with God, our family, our friends, and the community. Regrettably, there are individuals who hold the belief that they may engage in wrongdoing without consequence if their actions remain undetected. All sin, however, carries a consequence, and the ramifications of such actions will inevitably manifest themselves. The subject of this matter will be explored in the chapter titled, "Too Late." Jesus died to free us from the consequence of our sin. What specific consequence arises from this?

> Romans 6:23 "For the wages of sin is death, but the free gift
> of God is eternal life in Christ Jesus our Lord."

We understand that death, the cessation of our physical being, is not the sole consequence of sin; rather, it also entails spiritual and everlasting death. Some posit that the consequence of sin is everlasting punishment, involving torment in the flames of hell. I respectfully disagree. According to my understanding of scripture, the fate of the incorrigible sinner is complete and permanent non-existence. What characteristics distinguish an incorrigible sinner? An individual who disregards God's invitation and aspires to self-sufficiency will inevitably define their own morality, determining what constitutes good and evil. God's Kingdom offers no sanctuary to such individuals, and those who recognize God's grace but reject His sovereignty will find no reprieve. Those who have had the unfortunate experience of working for a strict and austere employer may understand the feeling, or the weight, of being treated like a slave. Therein lies the insidious nature of sin, which enslaves our lives.

> Romans 6:15-18 "What then? Are we to sin because we are
> not under law but under grace? By no means! 16 Do you not

know that if you present yourselves to anyone as obedient slaves, you are slaves of the one whom you obey, either of sin, which leads to death, or of obedience, which leads to righteousness? 17 But thanks be to God, that you who were once slaves of sin have become obedient from the heart to the standard of teaching to which you were committed, 18 and, having been set free from sin, have become slaves of righteousness."

Failing to grasp the importance of forgiveness places an extra weight upon us. Some contemporary Christians experience persistent feelings of guilt and shame due to past transgressions. Continued focus on past sins impedes the growth of forgiveness, love, joy, and peace in the spirit. When the Lord atoned for our sins, he completely absolved us of our transgressions. Only the blood of Christ can cleanse us from sin. No action on our part is necessary. Jesus has fully redeemed us through his sacrifice. If one were to habitually remind oneself of past failings, how might Jesus address such a situation? The crucifixion of Jesus atoned for all transgressions, both past and present. You have received the grace of God's forgiveness. Extend to yourself the gift of forgiveness.

Psalm 103:8-12 "The LORD is merciful and gracious, slow to anger and abounding in steadfast love. 9 He will not always chide, nor will he keep his anger forever. 10 He does not deal with us according to our sins, nor repay us according to our iniquities. 11 For as high as the heavens are above the earth, so great is his steadfast love toward those who fear him; 12 as far as the east is from the west, so far does he remove our transgressions from us."

The Lord has taken our sins and cast them as far away as the east is from the west. Do you know how far that is? Let's imagine a flight heading east for this experiment. Your eastward travels will continue indefinitely, and you will never arrive in the west. The concept of reaching a compass point west when traveling east, or vice versa, is impossible. A divide will always exist between east and west. God has completely forgiven our sins. This is a letter written by Paul, quoting from Jeremiah 31:34.

Hebrews 8:12 "For I will be merciful toward their iniquities, and I will remember their sins no more."

In the event of divine pardon, all sins are nullified and vanish completely. Through the blood of Christ, you are cleansed and now a Holy child of God. We have been released from the judge's condemnation. Freedom is a gift granted to us by God.

Romans 8:1 "There is therefore now no condemnation for those who are in Christ Jesus."

It is imperative that we actively replace any negative thoughts with this truth. Jesus has completely eradicated the sins of the past. We must cultivate a daily relationship with the Lord. Give that some thought. Christ's grace liberates us to experience his love, forgiveness, and inner peace, enabling us to replace negative thoughts with positive ones. Our struggle encompasses not only external forces but also the inner battles within our minds. We should find solace in the knowledge of God's love for us.

Acts 24:16 "So I always take pains to have a clear conscience toward both God and man."

Chapter twelve.

A is for Apprehension.

Fear is a weighty burden to carry. During his presidential inaugural address in 1933, Franklin D. Roosevelt stated:

> "So, first, let me assert my firm belief that the only thing we have to fear is ... fear itself — nameless, unreasoning, unjustified terror which paralyzes needed efforts to convert retreat into advance. In every dark hour of our national life a leadership of frankness and of vigor has met with that understanding and support of the people themselves which is essential to victory. And I am convinced that you will again give that support to leadership in these critical days."

That sentiment is a bold assertion, namely "the only thing we have to fear is fear itself." Fear is a God given preservation device to protect us from danger. There are two distinct types of fear: healthy and unhealthy. Unhealthy fear can function as a restrictive force, hindering our ability to push our boundaries. A healthy degree of fear serves as a cautionary signal in the face of potentially hazardous activities, such as skydiving, with apologies to all skydiving enthusiasts. Some people today express a fear of God. It possesses qualities that are both advantageous and disadvantageous. Let me elaborate on what I meant by that. Reverence for God implies acknowledging His supreme authority and being awestruck by His immense power. Reverence for God denotes our profound respect and highest esteem for Him. Having reverence for God brings a sense of tranquility, as we are assured of His love and unwavering protection. An unhealthy fear of God alienates individuals, fueled by the belief that God seeks to harm them. A significant number of individuals, unfortunately, remain estranged from divine love due to their perceived condemnation. A common source of fear regarding God stems from the conviction that submission to His will may limit personal autonomy and lead to consequences for one's actions. It's my belief and experience that were people to embrace the possibility of a divine presence; their fear would vanish without delay. Fear is a tool employed by Satan. He aims to evoke in us a sense of fear towards God. Instilling fear in the hearts of vulnerable individuals hinders their ability to hear God's message of love. The Holy Spirit's gift overcomes fear by instilling within us the empowering love of God.

> 1 John 4:18-19 "There is no fear in love, but perfect love casts out fear. For fear has to do with punishment, and whoever fears has not been perfected in love. 19 We love because he first loved us."

The five words we have just studied, each starting with the letter "A," will act as a substantial burden and obstruct our future happiness.

Chapter thirteen.

Rejection.

The numerous and varied activities that characterize modern life, including entertainment, work, and leisure pursuits, significantly impact our time allocation. It's possible that some individuals lack the desire to devote their time to the worship of God or the exploration of His word. They might perceive it as insignificant. During my time at Teacher's College in the 1980s, it was assured that widespread computer utilization would afford greater leisure time. The availability of computers, rather than reducing my workload, has paradoxically resulted in more time spent working on them. Despite our busy schedules, we consistently prioritize activities that we find enjoyable. We also allocate time for the pursuit of knowledge, whether it be formal academic studies leading to a degree, or professional development through on-the-job training or certification programs. Individuals habitually allocate time for pursuits that provide enjoyment or those deemed essential for enhancing their quality of life. It's a wonderful experience enjoying quality relationships with our children and grandchildren? We endeavor to schedule time for them. The connection shared with one's children provides significant fulfillment; however, as they mature, their lives become increasingly demanding, resulting in diminished opportunities for interaction. The formation of their own family, a natural progression after marriage, could lead to a reduction in the frequency of contact. We may see some members of our family once a year, usually for special occasions such as birthdays or other celebrations. It's disheartening when parental bonds weaken, but we don't expect children to prioritize our needs over time spent with their own families and friends. Their acknowledgement of our presence is a heartwarming gesture. Is it conceivable that God has similar sentiments towards us? It would be devastating if our children were to completely disown us; something that God would never do.

There is considerable uncertainty regarding the idea of divine retribution. It's crucial to understand that the concept of God in heaven, ready to punish wrongdoing immediately, is inaccurate. We must address and understand this issue right away. Divine commandments were not bestowed upon us as a means of securing salvation through adherence, nor condemnation through transgression. God's commands are not a form of entrapment. The commandments from God bring about peace and abundance. They are provided to ensure we have a fulfilling existence. Adherence to God's commandments would eliminate war, evil, and crime. The situation would yield both joy and security. Suffering is often a consequence of sin, or disobedience, to God's commands. Although we may not be directly responsible for the sin or offense, it invariably arises from transgression, which can be aptly defined as disobedience to the law of love. The presence of natural disasters and widespread sickness in the world today is attributed by some to the original sin, which they see as the source of a curse upon humanity. It wasn't the curse of God but the curse of the sin itself. The inclination to continue in sin is ultimately responsible for the suffering prevalent in the world today.

Genesis 3:17-19 "And to Adam he said, "Because you have listened to the voice of your wife and have eaten of the tree of which I commanded you, 'You shall not eat of it,' cursed is the ground because of you; in pain you shall eat of it all the days of your life; 18 thorns and thistles it shall bring forth for you; and you shall eat the plants of the field. 19 By the sweat of your face you shall eat bread, till you return to the ground, for out of it you were taken; for you are dust, and to dust you shall return."

God is informing them of the consequence of their sin, not a divine punishment from God. This was not the Father God's plan for His children. He provided them with all the necessary resources for a prosperous, happy, and fruitful existence. God's directive explicitly prohibited them from determining for themselves the nature of good and evil, symbolized by consuming the forbidden fruit. The standards for distinguishing between good and evil are established solely by God. Due to Adam and Eve's defiance of God's authority, they brought catastrophic consequences on themselves and future generations. Jesus came into the world to reconcile humankind with God, a task that only He could accomplish. Jesus stated that his mission was to bring redemption to sinners, liberating them from the consequences of their sinful conduct.

Mark 2:16-17 "And the scribes of the Pharisees, when they saw that he was eating with sinners and tax collectors, said to his disciples, "Why does he eat with tax collectors and sinners?" 17 And when Jesus heard it, he said to them, "Those who are well have no need of a physician, but those who are sick. I came not to call the righteous, but sinners."

The historical record consistently demonstrates the repercussions of the first human rebellion in the Garden of Eden and its ongoing nature, which have been expressed through acts of warfare and malevolence ever since. What additional hardships will we invite upon ourselves if we turn away from the Savior?

Hebrews 12:25 "See that you do not refuse him who is speaking. For if they did not escape when they refused him who warned them on earth, much less will we escape if we reject him who warns from heaven."

God the Father is not desirous of punishing us. We inflict punishment upon ourselves when we reject the Son of God, our Redeemer. God yearns for a deep connection with us, so much so that He sent His Son, Jesus, to suffer and die for us. He took the penalty we should have had, so we could have a life to come.

2 Peter 3:9 "The Lord is not slow to fulfill his promise as some count slowness, but is patient toward you, not wishing that any should perish, but that all should reach repentance."

What grounds could we have for declining such a promise? To repent is to undergo a shift in perspective, recognizing God's sovereignty in our lives, and actively seeking His direction.

1 Corinthians 2:14-15 "The natural person does not accept the things of the Spirit of God, for they are folly to him, and he cannot understand them because they are spiritually discerned. 15 The spiritual person judges all things, but is himself to be judged by no one."

Chapter fourteen.

Refusal.

Isaiah 30:1 "Ah, stubborn children," declares the LORD, "who carry out a plan, but not mine, and who make an alliance, but not of my Spirit, that they may add sin to sin"

Every individual exhibits a measurable degree of stubbornness; however, it's usually corrected when one acknowledges being wrong. Persistence in and of itself is not inherently negative. Persistence is essential when addressing complex issues. American football coach Chuck Noll said,

"Being stubborn is a virtue when you're right; it's only a character flaw when you're wrong."

So stubbornness can either help us or hinder us. We are steadfast and stubborn when we oppose unethical actions. However, an intractable stubbornness may lead to fatal consequences. It has been previously noted that some people assert they have a greater understanding than God. Despite the offer of everlasting life through Jesus Christ, these individuals believe they possess sufficient self-righteousness to merit entry into heaven. Self-righteous stubbornness does not bring salvation, but rather, it alienates us from God. God had to contend with an exceedingly stubborn Hebrew people during their liberation from slavery in Egypt. Notwithstanding the remarkable acts of deliverance orchestrated by God for the Israelites, they persisted in their stubborn refusal to follow his guidance.

2 Kings 17:13-18 Yet the LORD warned Israel and Judah by every prophet and every seer, saying, "Turn from your evil ways and keep my commandments and my statutes, under

all the Law that I commanded your fathers, and that I sent to you by my servants the prophets." 14 But they would not listen, but were stubborn, as their fathers had been, who did not believe in the LORD their God. 15 They despised his statutes and his covenant that he made with their fathers and the warnings that he gave them. They went after false idols and became false, and they followed the nations that were around them, concerning whom the LORD had commanded them that they should not do like them. 16 And they abandoned all the commandments of the LORD their God, and made for themselves metal images of two calves; and they made an Asherah and worshiped all the host of heaven and served Baal. 17 And they burned their sons and their daughters as offerings and used divination and omens and sold themselves to do evil in the sight of the LORD, provoking him to anger. 18 Therefore the LORD was very angry with Israel and removed them out of his sight. None was left but the tribe of Judah only.

Stubbornness can lead to an unhealthy focus on false gods, unattainable dreams. God will ignore individuals who ignore him. By stubbornly refusing to acknowledge God, we become susceptible to a multitude of sinful thoughts and actions, echoing the historical transgressions of the Israelites. There are three key objectives behind the recording of the Old Testament. The primary purpose is to lead us to Christ. Moreover, it serves as a stark reminder of humanity's rapid descent into evil and destruction when they disregard the Almighty's authority. Number three serves as a revelation for those who are willing to heed its message, revealing glimpses into the future. According to the New Testament, even those who have heard the word of salvation may become obstinate and oppose God.

Acts 19:1-9 And while Apollos was at Corinth, Paul passed through the inland country and came to Ephesus. There he found some disciples. 2 And he said to them, "Did you receive the Holy Spirit when you believed?" And they said, "No, we have not even heard that there is a Holy Spirit." 3 And he said, "Into what then were you baptized?" They said, "Into John's baptism." 4 And Paul said, "John baptized with the baptism of repentance, telling the people to believe in the one who was to come after him, Jesus." 5 On hearing this, they were baptized in the name of the Lord Jesus. 6 And when Paul had laid his hands on them, the Holy Spirit came on them, and they began speaking in tongues and prophesying. 7 There were about twelve men in all. 8 And he entered the synagogue and for three months spoke boldly, reasoning and persuading them about the kingdom of God. 9 But when some became stubborn and continued in unbelief, speaking evil of the Way before the congregation, he withdrew from them and took the disciples with him, reasoning daily in the hall of Tyrannus.

Stubbornness is a characteristic inherent to all of us. While this stance proves advantageous in resisting evil, it hinders us when we obstinately refuse God's authority. When we overcome recalcitrance, we gain access to the teachings of Jesus.

John 3:33-34 "Whoever receives his testimony sets his seal to this, that God is true. 34 For he whom God has sent utters the words of God, for he gives the Spirit without measure."

Chapter fifteen.

Let God be God!

Numbers 14:11 And the LORD said to Moses, "How long will this people despise me? And how long will they not believe in me, in spite of all the signs that I have done among them?

One might find the statement, "Let God be God" to be odd advice. God is attributed with the qualities of omnipotence, omniscience, and omnipresence, signifying infinite power, knowledge, and presence. Is therefore possible to prevent God from being God, if so in what way and how?

Psalm 103:19 "The LORD has established his throne in the heavens, and his kingdom rules over all."

He is the creator of all things and surpasses all things; how can we, the inhabitants of earth, prevent God from exercising His divine authority?

1 Chronicles 29:11-12 "Yours, O LORD, is the greatness and the power and the glory and the victory and the majesty, for all that is in the heavens and in the earth is yours. Yours is the kingdom, O LORD, and you are exalted as head above all. 12 Both riches and honor come from you, and you rule over all. In your hand are power and might, and in your hand, it is to make great and to give strength to all.

While the title of this book may appear absurd, even offensive, it's not intended to be so. We have the liberty to restrict God's authority since He has bestowed upon us the freedom to do so. The liberty to choose, a gift of immeasurable value from God to humanity. A liberty that grants individuals the option to reject God's presence in their lives. We have been bestowed with a free spirit by divine providence. Wouldn't you agree that this is intriguing? It's a testament to God's profound love for humankind that He refrains from dictating our choices.

The question that arises is whether Almighty God is the only God that you acknowledge. Is it possible that you have exchanged God for another god? The entity we serve, be it the Supreme Being or another god, constitutes our ultimate allegiance. That is remarkable! This is truly astounding! Allowing an authority other than God to govern our decisions implies a rejection of God's role as our guide. From the dawn of civilization, every society has adhered to a particular deity or pantheon. We heed and obey the deity, whatever form it may take, to whom we ascribe ultimate power. It's unfortunate that a great number of people today have chosen to worship a false god instead of the one true God. Though some deny the existence of a god, the object of their devotion is the entity they empower. Anything that acts as our ultimate guide and shapes our decisions essentially becomes a deity to us.

> Romans 6:16 "Do you not know that if you present yourselves to anyone as obedient slaves, you are slaves of the one whom you obey, either of sin, which leads to death, or of obedience, which leads to righteousness?"

The central question we face is identifying the highest authority in our individual lives. "I do not have a god in my life" is a frequent response from those who reject the idea of a divine creator when asked what guides them. If you want to find out who your god is, try answering these questions.

What authority determines the definition of right and wrong to you?
Who determines what is good and what is evil?
Who determines your moral values?
Who determines what is most important in your life?
Who sets the moral standards in your life?

If you respond with "me" to any of these question, it implies that you hold the belief that you are god. You have arrogantly elevated your position to a level equal with or even surpassing that of the divine. Assuming oneself to be the sole arbiter of morality directly contravenes the first commandment.

Exodus 20:3 "You shall have no other gods before me."

Any person or thing, including ourselves, that we elevate above God assumes a position of paramount importance in our lives. Those who deny the existence of God are vulnerable to the temptations of evil forces. Individuals who do not acknowledge the existence of a divine creator also reject the notion of Satan. That is precisely what Satan desires. He desires to avoid attracting attention to his presence. Satan's initial intention was to isolate humanity from its creator. The seeds of pride were planted in humanity by Satan. The pride that mirrors the character of Satan, past and present, serves as the ultimate undoing of mankind.

Isaiah 5:20-21 "Woe to those who call evil good and good evil, who put darkness for light and light for darkness, who put bitter for sweet and sweet for bitter! 21 Woe to those who are wise in their own eyes, and shrewd in their own sight!"

Chapter sixteen.

You are like God!

Psalm 82:6-7 I said, "You are gods, sons of the Most High, all of you; 7 nevertheless, like men you shall die, and fall like any prince."

It's predictable that those who deny the creator God will find the statement "you believe are God" unconvincing. When people determine their own morals, it implies they consider themselves superior to a higher authority. It's easy to mock the idea of people claiming god-like authority, but it's often surprisingly accurate. Let's go back to the Garden of Eden.

Planting the seed of corruption!
Let's glance at the ways Satan misled the first humans. We're all familiar with the narrative. God only prohibited eating from the tree of knowledge of good and evil, but he permitted them to eat all other fruits in the garden.

Genesis 2:15-17 "The LORD God took the man and put him in the garden of Eden to work it and keep it. 16 And the LORD God commanded the man, saying, "You may surely eat of every tree of the garden, 17 but of the tree of the knowledge of good and evil you shall not eat, for in the day that you eat of it you shall surely die."

Their death was not a punishment from God for their disobedience. Their defiance led to their death; in other words they brought death onto themselves. Performing this one task had fatal consequences. The fruit didn't kill them, so what did? We all have the liberty to make our own decisions. We will be solely responsible for any consequences that ensue. Although the fruit didn't bring death, the decision to choose for themselves what was good and what was evil led to their ultimate death. By what means? They elevated themselves above God and became a god unto themselves. Our inability to foresee the future prevents us from fully comprehending the detrimental outcomes of our actions. Human choices and deeds cause suffering and death, not by divine retribution. The serpent Satan knew that if Adam and Eve disobeyed God, they would die. He planned to plant seeds of uncertainty in the woman's thinking. That was only Satan's first step, for he knew that their disobedience would instill a pride in humanity that he possessed. Satan desired something beyond just ruining the bond between God and that first couple. Satan wanted to make sure that all the children born to them would die. The goal of Satan was to spread discord, first in the Garden, then throughout the thoughts of humankind. How did he achieve his goal? Satan created a lie and craftily introduced a damaging idea, a corrupting seed, which infected all of humanity's minds. We should revisit the location where our suffering first began.

Genesis 3:1-4 Now the serpent was more crafty than any other beast of the field that the LORD God had made. He said to the woman, "Did God actually say, 'You shall not eat of any tree in the garden'?" 2 And the woman said to the serpent, "We may eat of the fruit of the trees in the garden, 3 but God said, 'You shall not eat of the fruit of the tree that is in the midst of the garden, neither shall you touch it, lest you die.'" 4 But the serpent said to the woman, "You will not surely die."

It's false to say, "You will not surely die." This is how Jesus characterizes Satan, the devil, a liar from the beginning.

> John 8:44 "You are of your father the devil, and your will is to do your father's desires. He was a murderer from the beginning, and does not stand in the truth, because there is no truth in him. When he lies, he speaks out of his own character, for he is a liar and the father of lies."

Satan's fabrication was deliberate, designed not only to seal the fate of the first humans, but to establish a lasting influence upon their descendants. Have you become aware of the seed of deceit that Satan has sown in the hearts of humanity? Yes, that includes you and me.

> Genesis 3:4-5 But the serpent said to the woman, "You will not surely die. 5 For God knows that when you eat of it your eyes will be opened, and you will be like God, knowing good and evil."

A deliberate lie, and a temptation. Satan's deceit was claiming death wasn't definite, but we all know death comes to everyone. Satan tempted humans to think of themselves as gods, and they believed it. The temptation was strong. The whole thing was and remains purely in the mind. From this point forward, humankind has taken it upon itself to decide what's right and wrong, essentially becoming its own god. Despite lacking divine traits, humans frequently act as though they possess them, a misconception that has existed since the dawn of humanity. Do people today understand this deception?

> 2 Corinthians 11:3 "But I am afraid that as the serpent deceived Eve by his cunning, your thoughts will be led astray from a sincere and pure devotion to Christ."

Chapter seventeen.

Fruits of God's seed!

One of the most compelling elements of Christianity is this promise. Our calling is to be part of God's family, to be His children. The Son of God, Jesus, has made this possible by the grace of God.

> John 14:6 Jesus said to him, "I am the way, and the truth, and the life. No one comes to the Father except through me.

The seed implanted within the minds of humanity was a false representation of the seed Christ sows in the hearts of those who have faith. "You will become like God" the seed planted in the human psyche by Satan. Today we know that the word of God is the seed of Christ. Reading the entire parable in Matthew chapter 13 is highly recommended.

> Matthew 13:23 "As for what was sown on good soil, this is the one who hears the word and understands it. He indeed bears fruit and yields, in one case a hundredfold, in another sixty, and in another thirty."

The seed of God is the "word" of Christ. The seed of Christ grows and purifies the soul from the influence of Satan. The seed of Christ, the word, grows and bears much fruit, and we become children of God.

> Matthew 13:36-39 Then he left the crowds and went into the house. And his disciples came to him, saying, "Explain to us the parable of the weeds of the field." 37 He answered, "The one who sows the good seed is the Son of Man. 38 The field is the world, and the good seed is the sons of the

kingdom. The weeds are the sons of the evil one, 39 and the enemy who sowed them is the devil. The harvest is the end of the age, and the reapers are angels.

The path to everlasting life requires the establishment of a relationship with Jesus Christ, our Lord and Savior. That distinction differentiates Christianity from all other religious traditions. Most religions encompass beliefs in an everlasting existence, often called the afterlife. Excluding Christianity, all religious beliefs are founded on the principle of achieving salvation through deeds, with varying interpretations of what salvation means. Religion, in essence, prescribes a set of rules and regulations that must be followed to attain salvation. Conversely, Christianity holds an entirely different perspective. The acceptance of Jesus Christ as the Son of God grants Christians the gift of salvation, without the need for further works. In the absence of practical action, what constitutes the core tenets of Christianity? The reality of the situation is far more complex than the statement suggests. The Christian faith, in its nature, requires a more extensive explanation than any other religion. The character of our God is marked by a fondness for acts of virtue and benevolence.

John 5:17 "But Jesus answered them, "My Father is working until now, and I am working."

It's true that the Father and Jesus have never ceased to do good works. Many people believe God stopped working and rested on the Sabbath, that is the seventh day of the creation week. God doesn't need a rest. The biblical passage, "and God rested on the seventh day," signifies the completion of God's creative endeavor; God finished the creative work. He ceased active creation of the physical world, yet He continues to sustain all things. With the physical creation complete, God's attention turned to the sustenance of Adam and Eve and all other living creatures. God remained engaged with humankind, working to bring them closer to Him. What is the immediate significance of this for us? The meaning is profound, because God has destined us for a life of work, a life that holds immense promise.

> John 14:12 "Truly, truly, I say to you, whoever believes in me will also do the works that I do; and greater works than these will he do, because I am going to the Father."

It's truly an honor to be involved in the work of Jesus. This exerts a profound impact on our modern existence. In this present moment, Jesus is actively transforming believers to become integral parts of a greater work to come. Those who are faithful to God contribute to the holy mission. Positions of authority within the future Kingdom of God will be bestowed upon us. I hope that you are as excited about this as I am. The following scriptures explain the roles God has reserved for us, encompassing both our present life and the life to come, that is everlasting life in God's dominion. Recognizing our eagerness to embrace his magnificent grace, God, in his divine wisdom, ordained specific tasks for our fulfillment.

> Ephesians 2:10 "For we are his workmanship, created in Christ Jesus for good works, which God prepared beforehand, that we should walk in them."

This is excellent news. As saved Christians, we should be brimming with enthusiasm to fulfill the tasks God has entrusted to us.

> Titus 3:8 "The saying is trustworthy, and I want you to insist on these things, so that those who have believed in God may be careful to devote themselves to good works. These things are excellent and profitable for people."

The prospect of our future in God's kingdom fills me with overwhelming anticipation. Within the biblical text of the Revelation, Jesus Christ addresses letters to different churches. It's important to remember that this is the goal towards which we are being trained for today. If you are unfamiliar with this information, prepare to be surprised. Jesus writes a letter through the pen of John to the Church in Thyatira.

Revelation 2:25-27 "Only hold fast what you have until I come. 26 The one who conquers and who keeps my works until the end, to him I will give authority over the nations, 27 and he will rule them with a rod of iron, as when earthen pots are broken in pieces, even as I myself have received authority from my Father."

I am not currently prepared to assume authority over nations, and I am thankful for this divine opportunity to develop my moral compass and live righteously. Jesus speaks of a future period when he will return to earth as the King of God's kingdom. We shall reign with him over the nations, with the aim of bringing people to God the Father. The following scripture evokes a profound sense of awe and reverence due to the majesty and glory of God. This is the future promised to those who believe (the Saints).

1 Corinthians 6:2-3 "Or do you not know that the saints will judge the world? And if the world is to be judged by you, are you incompetent to try trivial cases? 3 Do you not know that we are to judge angels? How much more matters pertaining to this life!"

Those who belong to Christ will be bestowed with power over the world and angels. Not power as the authorities of this world, but as

God's representatives, we exercise judgment guided by righteousness. While our works do not earn us salvation, our salvation empowers us to engage in acts of goodness. We are divinely appointed to undertake this work.

Luke 19:17-19 And he said to him, 'Well done, good servant! Because you have been faithful in a very little, you shall have authority over ten cities.' 18 And the second came, saying, 'Lord, your mina has made five minas.' 19 And he said to him, 'And you are to be over five cities.'

Chapter eighteen.

The Temple.

1 Corinthians 15:3 "For I delivered to you as of first importance what I also received: that Christ died for our sins under the Scriptures."

A point of paramount importance must be highlighted in this discussion. From the beginning God knew the inevitable corruption of humanity by pride. God had foreseen the need for a redeemer to make atonement. God's inherent fairness requires that justice be served. There must be consequences for sin, mirrored in our laws against crime. The death of Jesus fulfilled God's justice, and his death paid for everyone's sins.

> Romans 5:8 "but God shows his love for us in that while we were still sinners, Christ died for us. 9 Since, therefore, we have now been justified by his blood, much more shall we be saved by him from the wrath of God. 10 For if while we were enemies we were reconciled to God by the death of his Son, much more, now that we are reconciled, shall we be saved by his life."

The "Tabernacle" and the "Temple" are frequently mentioned in the Old Testament. It's worth remembering that God had delivered Israel from their bondage in Egypt. Under Moses's guidance, God intended to lead them through the wilderness to the "promised land." The Tabernacle God commanded they build served as a place where God would meet with the priest. The location was designated for religious devotion. The Tabernacle served as a constant reminder of God's presence. The tabernacle contained a consecrated inner sanctum known as the Holy of Holies. This is the place where the Ark of the

Covenant was enshrined. Once a year, this location served as the exclusive site for the priest's meeting with God. Within the sanctuary, the priest encountered the Divine presence at the mercy seat. The priest presenting blood as a propitiation for the transgressions of the people.

> Hebrews 9:6 "These preparations having thus been made, the priests go regularly into the first section, performing their ritual duties, 7 but into the second (most Holy place) only the high priest goes, and he but once a year (atonement), and not without taking blood, which he offers for himself and for the unintentional sins of the people."

The profound sacredness of this ritual is underscored by the deep spiritual significance inherent in all Holy Days, including this recorded Day of Atonement. This annual day of atonement was predicting the atoning sacrifice and redemption that we have in Jesus Christ. The Tabernacle served as the designated location where God manifested his presence and interacted with the people.

> Exodus 40:34-38 "Then the cloud covered the tent of meeting, and the glory of the LORD filled the tabernacle. 35 And Moses could not enter the tent of meeting because the cloud settled on it, and the glory of the LORD filled the tabernacle. 36 Throughout all their journeys, whenever the cloud was taken up from over the tabernacle, the people of Israel would set out. 37 But if the cloud was not taken up, then they did not set out till the day that it was taken up. 38 For the cloud of the LORD was on the tabernacle by day, and fire was in it by night, in the sight of all the house of Israel throughout all their journeys."

The presence of God in the Tabernacle was made evident through the manifestation of a cloud. The appearance of the cloud signified God's dwelling among the people. Following the lifting of the cloud, the people were led through the wilderness by it. Is there a discernible connection between this and our lives?

Following their settlement in Jerusalem, the Israelites, under the reign of Solomon, ultimately constructed a Temple dedicated to God. This temple was constructed from blocks of stone. Compared to the Tabernacle it superseded, the Temple offered a more enduring architectural presence. The Temple's holiest chamber, meticulously built, was where the priest engaged in communion with God and presented the blood of atonement as an offering. Is there a role for a Temple in our lives today?

> 1 Corinthians 3:16-17 "Do you not know that you are God's temple and that God's Spirit dwells in you? 17 If anyone destroys God's temple, God will destroy him. For God's temple is holy, and you are that temple."

The Tabernacle in the wilderness and the Temple in Jerusalem were a foreshadow of something greater to come. Through these events, God's future actions in the end times were being foreshadowed, especially for the faithful. The Temple in Jerusalem was destroyed in 70 AD by the Roman general Titus. The necessity of the Temple has ceased, for the Spirit of God now dwells within each of us. Our hearts and minds now serve as channels for God's love. Today we meet with God in our hearts through the Spirit. Drawing parallels to the Israelites' journey through the wilderness, the Holy Spirit guides us through the trials and tribulations that we encounter. The Temple was revered as a place of holiness.

Ezekiel 44:4-8 "Then he brought me by way of the north gate to the front of the temple, and I looked, and behold, the glory of the LORD filled the temple of the LORD. And I fell on my face. 5 And the LORD said to me, "Son of man, mark well, see with your eyes, and hear with your ears all that I shall tell you concerning all the statutes of the temple of the LORD and all its laws. And mark well the entrance to the temple and all the exits from the sanctuary. 6 And say to the rebellious house, to the house of Israel, Thus says the Lord GOD: O house of Israel, enough of all your abominations, 7 in admitting foreigners, uncircumcised in heart and flesh, to be in my sanctuary, profaning my temple, when you offer to me my food, the fat and the blood. You have broken my covenant, in addition to all your abominations. 8 And you have not kept charge of my holy things, but you have set others to keep my charge for you in my sanctuary."

A reminder that the Temple of the Holy Spirit which is our body, must remain undefiled by abominations, idols, and the moral standards of this secular world.

2 Corinthians 6:16-18 "What agreement has the temple of God with idols? For we are the temple of the living God; as God said, "I will make my dwelling among them and walk among them, and I will be their God, and they shall be my people. 17 Therefore go out from their midst, and be separate from them, says the Lord, and touch no unclean thing; then I will welcome you, 18 and I will be a father to you, and you shall be sons and daughters to me, says the Lord Almighty."

We are privileged to receive a truly wonderful gift from our Father. He is present within us through the power of the Spirit. As the Temple, we cannot house two deities. Persisting in the belief of a self-righteous, proud, and defiant deity represents a rejection of the true God and His son, Jesus. We should strive to move beyond the tendency to act solely on our individual mindsets, a tendency mirrored in the act of consuming from the tree of good and evil. It is imperative that we avoid dictating our own moral principles. It is imperative that we acknowledge God's supremacy in every aspect of our being.

Romans 8:8-9 "Those who are in the flesh cannot please God. 9 You, however, are not in the flesh but in the Spirit, if in fact the Spirit of God dwells in you. Anyone who does not have the Spirit of Christ does not belong to him."

Chapter nineteen.

Is it too late?

John 3:3 Jesus answered him, "Truly, truly, I say to you, unless one is born again he cannot see the kingdom of God."

I acknowledge that a substantial portion of this book's audience identifies as Christian. It is my sincere desire that this book be read among atheists and agnostics, as time is becoming increasingly limited. A warning is issued by Jesus for all. Be on the alert, because his return is imminent, soon he will gather his followers, the Saints together. What becomes of individuals who choose not to accept God's gracious offer of salvation? Jesus stated that a spiritual rebirth is necessary to see, meaning to enter the Kingdom. There is but one path for salvation, and that it is solely by the grace of God, through Jesus Christ. Performing good deeds does not excuse one from responsibility. It's essential for people to undergo a spiritual renewal, a rebirth emanating from God the Father. It's imperative that people acknowledge Jesus Christ as their savior and receive the Holy Spirit. For those suffering from any one or all the five A words, time is running out. Jesus implores all to repent and seek divine guidance. The word "repent" is derived from the Greek term "metanoia," which denotes a transformation in one's mindset, a complete shift in perspective. Let go of apathy, relinquish arrogance, suppress anger, shed the anchor, do not fear, and replace them with the love and forgiveness of God, as manifested through Jesus the Messiah. Saving us has been God's eternal purpose.

2 Peter 3:9 "The Lord is not slow to fulfill his promise as some count slowness, but is patient toward you, not wishing that any should perish, but that all should reach repentance."

The appointed time is fast approaching. It's imperative to understand that the tribulation will leave no room for recourse once it begins. Individuals who embrace Christianity during the tribulation period will face severe persecution. Upon the conclusion of the tribulation, the reign of Jesus will begin on Earth. Scriptural accounts describe a period of one thousand years, during which Christ reigns with the resurrected saints, culminating in the creation of a new heaven and earth. A judgment before the great white throne occurs immediately prior to the universal restoration. The ultimate judgment of those who reject the Lord in this life will be based on their actions and omissions.

Revelation 20:11-15 "Then I saw a great white throne and him who was seated on it. From his presence earth and sky fled away, and no place was found for them. 12 And I saw the dead, great and small, standing before the throne, and books were opened. Then another book was opened, which is the book of life. And the dead were judged by what was written in the books, according to what they had done. 13 And the sea gave up the dead who were in it, Death and Hades gave up the dead who were in them, and they were judged, each one of them, according to what they had done. 14 Then Death and Hades were thrown into the lake of fire. This is the second death, the lake of fire. 15 And if anyone's name was not found written in the book of life, he was thrown into the lake of fire."

Through Christ alone can forgiveness of sins be obtained, and it's imperative that we turn to him and experience spiritual rebirth. The names of those who are reborn are inscribed in the Book of Life. They are destined for everlasting life. It's my hope that all individuals will repent and seek God's forgiveness before they face judgment for their transgressions.

> Revelation 22:11-15 "Let the evildoer still do evil, and the filthy still be filthy, and the righteous still do right, and the holy still be holy." 12 "Behold, I am coming soon, bringing my recompense with me, to repay each one for what he has done. 13 I am the Alpha and the Omega, the first and the last, the beginning and the end." 14 Blessed are those who wash their robes, so that they may have the right to the tree of life and that they may enter the city by the gates. 15 Outside are the dogs and sorcerers and the sexually immoral and murderers and idolaters, and everyone who loves and practices falsehood."

Conclusion.

A common plea amongst Christians is for the spiritual enlightenment of their fellow human beings, urging them to welcome the Lord into their hearts. The briefness of life necessitates the understanding that our time is finite. At the time of our judgment before God, we will be called upon to give a thorough explanation for all our choices and decisions, recognizing that none of us have a perfect past. Disconnected from God, we are lost in the sea of life, yet a significant number remain ignorant of the wonderful promise we have in the Lord.

The ultimate reward of Paradise awaits those who embrace God's direction in their lives. While we strive forward without direction, our internal voice lacks the wisdom to lead us to paradise. We are grateful for God's guidance, which is like the wind filling our sails, leading us safely to God's Kingdom. The sail represents the Word of God. He possesses the sole authority to distinguish between good and evil. Only God possesses the ability to guide us on our journey through this tumultuous sea. The power of the Holy Spirit is the impetus that drives us forward, leading us to everlasting life in God's realm of paradise. How do you perceive Jesus? By what means does Jesus deliver us from the hazards of the wild sea? Jesus gives us both the sail and the wind. He embodies God's word, serving as our Shepherd and teacher. Jesus magnificently proclaimed the gospel as he journeyed through the dusty roads of Judea and Samaria.

John 3:36 "Whoever believes in the Son has eternal life; whoever does not obey the Son shall not see life, but the wrath of God remains on him."

We are directed to have faith in and follow the teachings of Jesus. If we truly love the Lord, our desire will be to obey his will, not the dictates of our own internal desires.

John 14:15-18 "If you love me, you will keep my commandments. 16 And I will ask the Father, and he will give you another Helper, to be with you forever, 17 even the Spirit of truth, whom the world cannot receive, because it neither sees him nor knows him. You know him, for he dwells with you and will be in you. 18 "I will not leave you as orphans; I will come to you.

We are not isolated in the face of this unpredictable sea. Jesus did not abandon us to our own devices when it comes to salvation. Our world is fraught with difficulties, and a substantial number of false teachers operate within it. They may appear angelic, but their actions reveal a sinister agenda. Through the Holy Spirit, we are given discernment, and our decisions are directed by the Word of God.

Ephesians 4:10-16 "He who descended is the one who also ascended far above all the heavens, that he might fill all things.) 11 And he gave the apostles, the prophets, the evangelists, the shepherds and teachers, 12 to equip the saints for the work of ministry, for building up the body of Christ, 13 until we all attain to the unity of the faith and of the knowledge of the Son of God, to mature manhood, to the measure of the stature of the fullness of Christ, 14 so that we may no longer be children, tossed to and fro by the waves and carried about by every wind of doctrine, by human cunning, by craftiness in deceitful schemes. 15 Rather, speaking the truth in love, we are to grow up in every way into him who is the head, into Christ, 16 from whom the whole body, joined and held together by every joint with which it is equipped, when each part is working properly, makes the body grow so that it builds itself up in love."

We are God's children, and there is only one God. Those who seek God become children of the Most High.

Ephesians 3:14-19 "For this reason I bow my knees before the Father, 15 from whom every family in heaven and on earth is named, 16 that according to the riches of his glory he may grant you to be strengthened with power through his Spirit in your inner being, 17 so that Christ may dwell in your hearts through faith—that you, being rooted and grounded in love, 18 may have strength to comprehend with all the saints what is the breadth and length and height and depth, 19 and to know the love of Christ that surpasses knowledge, that you may be filled with all the fullness of God.

Our existence is characterized by a constant struggle. Our conflict is not only against physical adversaries but also against spiritual forces of wickedness in the heavenly realms. The fight is justified, as our internal voices will endeavor to impede our progress towards a closer relationship with God. The victory of Jesus is undeniable. He has escaped from the clutches of death. Our objective is to eliminate the influence of the devil and cultivate a divine presence within our hearts and minds. As long as we are alive, it's never too late to act. What motivated the masses to follow Jesus? His message brought hope and the promise of a glorious existence after death. The message offers a new perspective, enriching the lives of all who receive it. A joyful experience that contributes to the current quality of our existence.

Did you love *Let God be God!*? Then you should read *Will you go to Heaven*[1] by Brian William Warburton!

The question of life after death usually gets asked at funerals. Many people believe that there is life after death. We are comforted when we hear that our deceased loved one has gone to heaven. This book is a short study into that very subject. Do we go to heaven when we die? In this book we will study the subject of heaven, where heaven is situated. Will we go there in spirit when we die, are we good enough to go to heaven? What happens to our bodies, will they live again in another form? When Jesus was resurrected, it was a bodily resurrection, will our resurrection be the same? Where do non-believers go, do they get a chance to enter heaven? What is our final destination, is it heaven or

---

1. https://books2read.com/u/mdXeRO

2. https://books2read.com/u/mdXeRO

some other place? Importantly, what will we be doing there in our final destination?

Also by Brian William Warburton

Saved by the Word
Will you go to Heaven
Let God be God!
Crown of Thorns!
Why Does God Allow Suffering?
Jerusalem 2025
Jerusalem 2025

www.ingramcontent.com/pod-product-compliance
Lightning Source LLC
Chambersburg PA
CBHW051757130726
47987CB00003B/1011